The Invisible Parenting Handbook

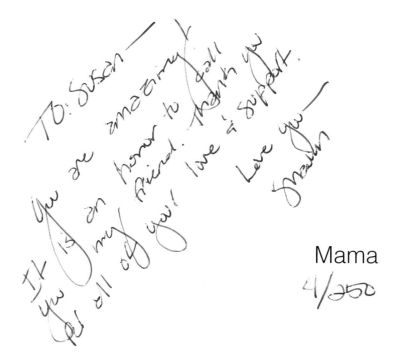

To: Susan —

You are amazing! It is an honor to call you my friend. Thank you for all of your love & support.

Love you

Mama

4/250

First Edition, Limited Run November 2013

All of Us Productions
PO Box 77207
Seattle WA 98177
www.allofusproductions.com

Printed in the United States of America
First Printing 2013
ISBN 978-0615923154

This book is dedicated to you, Carly.

"Your children are not your children. They are the sons and daughters of Life's longing for itself. They come through you but not from you, and though they are with you yet they belong not to you."—Kahlil Gibran

Table of Contents

Illustrations by Carly

     Pages 4, 6, 34, 43, 47, 54, 65, 80, 89, 92, 121, 140, 148, 154, 158, 172, 178, 181, 185, 187, 201, 206 (and the front cover)

Acknowledgements

Okay, so I guess I should come clean right from the start. As a salesperson I have the gift of finding support in the most amazing places and from the most generous people. Friends, colleagues, family, and strangers jump in to help me complete projects and meet crazy deadlines. I must have learned how to find the help I needed from selling airplane parts, where the customers are always in a huge hurry. I received the same level of assistance with this book. From the moment the idea grabbed me, people started offering to help. Later, as the book took shape, and everyone realized the enormity of time and effort involved, these folks held fast. Thanks very much to all of you for hanging in there to the finish. You did a brilliant job, and I can never find the words to tell you how touched and deeply grateful I am. I owe you all big time!

I believe it takes a village to raise a child, and it took a village to write this book. I'm dyslexic and writing is no picnic, but for four years this concept wouldn't let me go. At first I fought the idea, but I finally gave in and sat down at the computer. I was amazed. The words just flowed through me! Still, the initial result was pretty scattered. As I told someone the other day, without the help I received from my community, this book would have been the literary equivalent to a Jackson Pollack painting. (And, I don't mean that in a good way.) My team of supporters inspired, prodded, and encouraged me; surrounded me with love and friendship; reviewed, edited, proofread, and offered me many of the pearls of wisdom I've included throughout this book.

My good friend and neighbor Susan pushed me for years to write this book. Without her encouragement and insistence, I might never have finished... or even started. Once I made the decision to dive into this project, my dear friend Lacey stepped forward to create a rigorous schedule, one she made sure I followed. Everyone needs a Lacey in their life! Not only did these two lovely women jumpstart this book, but they also reviewed the early, rough—and I mean really rough—draft. I took their insightful suggestions, then passed the second draft of the manuscript along to my larger community of family and friends. My heartfelt thanks to you both.

Many kind friends reviewed the second draft. Jon, my boss, was the first to get back to me, responding in fewer than twenty-four hours. Jon, thank goodness for your kindness and speed. You spared me from having to sit on pins and needles for too long. My friend Sandy, who encouraged me from the get-go, offered spot-on feedback. Shirley Enebrad, an author and my friend, gave great suggestions and asked questions that really made me think. Wendy, my big-hearted sister-in-law let me know where the book touched her heart and helped inspire her parenting. Paula Brody, another author and friend, helped me see the manuscript from a non-parent's perspective. Deep appreciation to Salina, for her honesty and tenacity about making suggestions she felt would help the book but might hurt my feelings. Don't worry. My feelings are intact! Jenny, who has always been willing to lend a helping hand, jumped in to review the second draft. Last, but never least, Stephanie, who keeps my husband's office running like clockwork and has become part of our family, I'm so grateful for the time you took to comment. Thanks to all of you!

After revising, I handed off the manuscript to my editor, Kelly Malone, who, after working her magic, sent the first edited version back to me. Kelly, the best professional editor ever, is amazingly skilled. She helped make this book cohesive and much more readable. As our neighbor of sixteen years, Kelly knew how to fill in the blanks. Still, she had lots of questions and suggestions, so we spent hours on the phone reviewing questions and changes, while I traveled up and down the state going to and from meetings. This book truly has been a collaborative effort. Thanks for a best seller, Kelly. Here's to your upcoming book.

At this point, my husband, Mark, and I spent a lovely, rainy Sunday sitting in our living room, while he read the manuscript to me out loud. Mark, what an awesome gift to hear you read about Carly's childhood and for me to see how certain portions touched you so deeply. After that reading, I revised the manuscript again, and when my eyes, heart, and soul couldn't take any more, I handed it back to Kelly for another round of edits. She and her husband, Tom, dug deep, reworking and polishing, until it was ready for me to review again.

Then there's the fabulous five. These reviewers provided support and a fresh pair of eyes to the final draft, helping to make sure the copy was clean and error-free. Salina jumped back in wholeheartedly. Love that focus! Jenny also dove back in with a sharp eye and perceptive questions. My wonderful customer Jeremy suggested some invaluable reorganization. Michal provided her gift at finding undotted i's and uncrossed t's along with her knack for revising an awkward phrase or passage into one that flowed smoothly. Bridget asked thought-provoking questions throughout the manuscript. (She also took me on a hike before she reviewed the manuscript to explain how important cairns are to finding the way along a path, especially the path of parenting.) I know you all got more than you bargained for during this eye-straining, mind-numbing review. Thanks for sticking it out!

Throughout this process, my mom offered her memories, wisdom, and unwavering support. Carol, my dear friend and walking buddy, listened to my ramblings and helped guide me about which stories to put in and which to toss out. And Jeremy, my delightful customer, gave his time and provided some of the stories in this book.

During the time my dear circle of friends were reviewing the manuscript, another friend approached me, asking to buy one of the hardbound special editions of this book. Thank you, Dan, for your inspiration! As a result, I emailed my friends and family, asking how many were interested in buying a book and adding their hearts (and checks) to my circle of support. The orders kept coming in. Your generosity allowed me to contract with a printer for a run of two-hundred-fifty limited editions.

And wouldn't you just know that I already knew the perfect person to help with that printing. Steve, who has been my printer and friend for more than twenty years, made it possible to run the first edition. He and his wife, Cheryl, found creative ways to bring this book to life. Bridget's friend Ben and my friend Carol, helped with the cover ideas and font for the book. And Aix Battoe, graphic designer extraordinaire, came to the rescue to help me meet a very hard deadline. Thank you all for shepherding my manuscript to print.

And now, Blythe Pelham. Boy, am I lucky to have such a great sister. Blythe played a dual role in this project. Not only did she copy edit the final draft, but when our deadline changed and we were scrambling, she came to the rescue to format this book. Blythe, I can't tell you how much I appreciate your artistic touch and puzzle-solving. You saved my arse. You've always been good at that.

Mark, you're the best. You know I could go on for days, but I just want to say this—you're my greatest supporter, my rock, and the person who helps keep my toes in the earth and my feet on the planet.

And then of course there's Carly. Most especially, Carly! Traveling on this path with you has made our lives so much richer. You also enriched the book with your drawings. The cover artwork and the illustrations added such joy, depth, and beauty. Thank you for helping me make this book a reality. I trust you will treasure it for years to come.

The Many Paths of Parenting

I wrote this book for you, Carly, and for your family, should you choose to have one. I wrote it for you as though I were writing a letter—a really long letter—because that was the easiest and most honest way for me to convey my feelings and capture the experiences we've had together. As I wrote, I thought others might benefit from our experiences, so I wanted to share our stories by putting my letter into a book. I'm grateful for how open you were to the idea, and for creating all the artwork in this book. As much as we taught you, you taught us, so it seems perfect that we worked on it together.

As I was finishing this book, and my friend Bridget was about to do the last round of edits, she had an inspiration and insisted we make the one-hour drive from Seattle to hike Mount Pilchuck. She wanted me to see the cairns, the man-made rock piles that mark the way along the path. As she, her young son, Jack, her friend, Jodie, and I hiked, Bridget told me she hoped my book would help others see that the parenting path can be both wide and narrow, rocky, and often steep. And if you watch carefully, you might just see very subtle cairns that point the way.

As we climbed, we couldn't find any cairns. We passed a group of strangers walking down the hill. We asked them about the absence of cairns. One of them, Nick, gave us a nod and a wink, and said, "Look closer on your way down." Thank you Nick, our new-found friend, for your kind, quick thinking and for the lovely cairns you put out for us (and especially for Jack) to see when we followed the path down the mountain. Every single one of them made us smile. Carly, along your life's path, I trust you'll find folks like Nick, people who spread joy, and care about making the world a better place, people who will generously share their wisdom, time, and talents. Some of these folks will help you find your way. Take note of the advice that works for you and let go of the stuff that doesn't, including the tips I've written in this book.

One more thing. To share this book with a larger audience, I've explained some experiences and named some people in your life as though you aren't familiar with them. When I talk about my sister, I write, "my sister (your aunt Blythe)." Or when I write about the trips you took in high school, I describe them. These descriptions are for the benefit of those reading this book. I hope you'll bear with me.

So here we go, Carly.

Becoming Visible

Remember when you were a little girl and you didn't like some of the rules we laid down for you? When I told you that bedtime was at 7:30 and you said that you weren't tired and I told you that this was a non-negotiable rule? I told you the rule was important because your health depended on a full night's sleep. Taking a nap was another important rule from this life-saving parenting guide. You didn't always like or understand why you had to take a nap. You'd question and cry about this rule. But I learned quickly that if you didn't have a rest midday or were lacking sleep, nothing could move forward with ease for any of us. So nap time was non-negotiable.

And, yet another rule. If you're using your outside voice, go outside. I gave you tips from this book, such as using your inside voice when you were inside, because it's important to consider those around you. And when you asked me where I came up with those rules and tips, remember I told you I found them in The Invisible Parenting Handbook?

Someday, I explained to you, when you became a parent the handbook would become visible to you. Well guess what kiddo, this is my version of that handbook. You know how I feel about empty promises, so I wanted to write down these rules and tips while I still remembered them.

Your dad and I believed that it was our job to help you grow by letting you stretch and explore while bumping into the firm boundaries we created, hoping to keep you safe (as much as possible) while learning about the world. We knew that some of who you are would be determined by hardwiring while other traits would be learned, gathered, and enhanced by our guidance and the guidance of others.

Here are some of the qualities that we felt you would need on this trip through life.

HONESTY INTEGRITY COMPASSION
RESPECT FOR YOURSELF & OTHERS
RESPONSIBILITY CONFIDENCE
SELF-SUFFICIENCY AUTHENTICITY
OF SERVICE TO YOUR COMMUNITY
PASSION CURIOSITY
COURAGE
MANNERS, WORLD STEWARDSHIP
FAITH ABILITY TO DIG
CAPACITY FOR CONVERSATION D
& ability TO LISTEN E
APTITUDE TO FIND OR IN A STORM E
HEEDING THE OF OTHERS P
WISDOM
OPENNESS SATISFACTION
GRATITUDE

Our goal for you was that you would know how to feed your soul, care for and nourish your body, educate your mind with critical thinking, and listen to your intuition. We felt that the more tools (such as the qualities on the list) you had in your toolbox, the more paths you'd be equipped to follow.

Your dad and I didn't write down these qualities, we just talked about them, and agreed on them. When you were about six months old, we began writing down our ideas, goals, and hopes. We started the list when we asked our friend Richard to be your godfather and take care of you if something happened to us. He immediately agreed, as long as we wrote down a list of our priorities for you, so that he could honor our wishes . . . just in case.

He asked for a list of twenty do's and don'ts. It took us some time and plenty of conversation to compile this list. When we were done, Richard put the list in an envelope, sealed the envelope with wax, and said he hoped he would never have to open it. Thankfully for all of us, he didn't. Richard gave us such a gift by asking us to create that list, which helped us pin down all we hoped for your life.

We'd both met so many parents who tried to make up for their own strict or harsh upbringing by taking it easy on their kids and not laying down rules. Well, guess what? Life has rules. And some are really lousy. But you've got to learn to live with them or decide if moving a rule or boundary is worth the consequence. When we created the list for Richard, we came up with rules we felt would enable you to learn the qualities we thought would help you in life. And they have. Those qualities you learned as a result of our dreams, goals, and the resulting rules, have enabled you to explore options that many of your peers who've grown up without rules aren't able to.

This is our Carly List.

Maintain connections with the important people in Carly's life for continuity and to build a solid foundation of community

Assign chores for responsibility

Make sure she savors childhood, so she doesn't grow up too fast

Have her work part-time jobs for clothes, college savings, and fun

- Avoid spoiling Carly with big-ticket items such as cars, to teach her the value of honest work and a dollar
- Steer clear of junk TV and junk food
- Promote reading—very important
- Allow no video games
- Take vacations together
- Make sure there are plenty of positive influences in Carly's life
- Teach her to have fun and be responsible about safety, without becoming frightened of risks
- Instill manners so that she can travel in any circle comfortably
- Encourage participation in sports, if she's interested
- Limit the use of cosmetics
- Veto unreasonable clothing or jewelry
- Instill spiritual values (not religious)
- Follow through on thank you notes

While writing this book, I realized a few more core values that we followed as you were growing up, and I would have added to the list:

- *Talk with each other. Hold meaningful conversations.*

- *Develop moral values and social awareness.*

- *Foster a sense of gratitude for what you have rather than entitlement to what you don't have.*

Richard's request was an inspiration. Our list became more than a laundry list of do's and don'ts. It became the roadmap that we followed for the next eighteen years. Thinking back, it might have been handy to have a copy of that list on the fridge or someplace where we could all see it every day. That way, we wouldn't forget what we'd set out to do and we could make sure we stayed on track.

On your eighteenth birthday, Richard surprised us all by giving you his copy of our list. What a wonderful surprise! I'm so glad he gave us this amazing gift. We certainly accomplished some of the items better than others, but we were deeply moved to see how much you embody so many of the values we'd hoped to instill. That said, clearly we didn't do everything perfectly or even correctly. I haven't met anyone who has, and I don't think perfection is the point of life. We did our best, and I think we became better parents as we went along.

Do you remember when you were four and we brought your foster brother into our family? Well I do. He was with us for two years, from when he was seven until he was nine. Parenting your foster brother helped us grow as parents, quickly. We went to many counselors with your brother. One counselor suggested a great book—*Giving the Love that Heals* by Harville Hendrix. I read the book, which was such a gift, and shared what I learned with your dad.

What I learned pushed me to become a clearer, more efficient, and better parent. I learned how to avoid letting my own childhood get in the way of yours or your brother's. My lessons in life have come from places of pain as well as places of joy. And, they're my lessons. If they help you, great. If we can't get past them, and they interfere with our being a good parent, that's another story. I trust your lessons will come from pain and joy too. Continuous learning is one of the points to life.

As you know, I think most of us have been on this earth many times. My personal goal is to grow in every way possible so that next time I'll get new lessons. I also think we have a destination but we have many choices about which paths we take to get there. As I've always said to you, "Make good choices." Carly, it's my wish that you follow paths that are safe and healthy for you as well as others and along the way you can help the world to become a better place for all.

I trust you'll enjoy reminiscing about your childhood as you read this book, and I'm sure that your memories of the past will be different from mine. Just remember to hold on to what fits best for you.

Autobiographical Snapshots

I had a tough childhood, which is why choosing to become a parent was such an enormous decision for me. I wanted to make sure that I made the choice to parent for sound reasons and was ready to give it my all. Carly, it was super important for me to make sure that you didn't have a painful childhood like I did, and that you didn't have to relive my childhood because I didn't find the methods to heal myself before giving birth to you which could have carried on the chain of abuse. So I thought it might be useful to review my childhood memories. Some of these stories you may have already heard, but I want you to have as full of a picture as possible before you read more of this book. As you know, learning from the mistakes and successes of the past can help us build better futures.

The following stories are snapshots, bits and pieces of my history that occurred during the years from childhood into adulthood. I know that my memories are just that—mine. Not my mother's, not my fathers' (either father—biological or adoptive), not my siblings'. Obviously, I'm telling the stories from my perspective. My point of view of these events has everything to do with my age at the time and the lens I looked through.

Surviving

As you know, my mom and dad divorced when I was about four years old. My sister (your aunt Blythe) and I lived with my mom (Grandma Carol). Your grandma Carol married Grandpa Lin when I was five. After they married, my mom, my biological dad (Grandpa J.), and my new stepdad thought it would be best if Lin adopted Auntie Blythe and me. Our family knew we'd be moving for Lin's job and wouldn't visit my biological dad very often, plus it would be easier for us kids if we all shared the same last name, and Lin wanted to take care of us which would relieve my dad of paying child support. It just seemed to make sense at the time. Although, thinking back, my dad's agreement to let Lin adopt us left some scars. With divorce there's often a sense of abandonment but Grandpa J.'s giving me up for adoption intensified that feeling.

Blythe didn't want the adoption and has her own story to tell. In a nutshell, she didn't want Lin to adopt her and she said so in court. When her first marriage ended, she changed her name to what it had been before Lin adopted her.

On the other hand, I was all for it! I was small and it didn't scare me to have a new dad. Though we had a rocky time, in the end my stepfather taught me many lessons I needed to learn in this lifetime. It's why I think we were together. When you were born, Carly, we made peace. And now that he's passed over, I miss him.

Grandpa Lin had two kids from a prior marriage, Christopher and Susun. When he and your grandma married, your uncle Christopher was about eighteen and away at college. Your aunt Susun was fourteen. When Susun was sixteen, her mother died of cancer and then she came to live with us. Christopher would come home to visit on summer breaks. When he graduated from college, he also babysat for long weekends. We always had a blast when he babysat. Auntie Susun was a great babysitter too. I loved my instant siblings.

Blended families can present challenges, and ours was no different. As a result, my childhood was a bit of a roller coaster. Most of the time my parents were working really hard at making their marriage work so they were often walking on egg shells to avoid problems which made life a bumpy road for all involved.

Also, your grandma Carol and grandpa Lin had very different parenting styles. When the pressure got to be too much, Grandpa lashed out at me. He was emotionally, verbally, and sometimes physically abusive. I was a strong-willed child. He had to take his rage out on someone and I guess he thought I was the best target. I think he thought I was tough and could take the abuse without crumbling. On the other hand, when he abused me, my strong will angered him further increasing the intensity of his assaults. I fought back by not showing him any weakness. My refusal to give in made his "need" to break my spirit even stronger, which was ironic since he seemed to choose me because I wouldn't break.

To others, it may not have seemed I was breaking but they soon realized I was. One night, when I was seven or eight, and the abuse had been going on for a couple years, I experienced a strange hallucination. I honestly don't remember this event (Grandma and Uncle Christopher told me about it years later), but it was a turning point for the family. Christopher was home from school and our family had gone out to dinner. While we were eating, I looked up and I saw people coming out of the walls. I told my mom and Christopher what I saw. How could those people walk through walls?? Because I blocked my experience, I have no idea if my father or sisters overheard the conversation or remember the event. We never talked about it, and I have no idea why.

I don't know if Uncle Christopher ever saw Grandpa Lin abuse me. I know Grandma Carol had. But it took that night at the restaurant for her to realize the profound impact his abuse had on me. Christopher must have had an idea what had been going on, or maybe my mother or I told him, because after dinner he told mom that she had to get Grandpa Lin to stop abusing me (which she did, although his verbal abuse continued. It just seemed to be part of his personality.) Talking with him was extremely intense for everyone. Grandpa Lin was exceptionally intelligent. He had a photographic memory and he was very proud of the fact that he'd graduated from Harvard. There was no way anyone could win an argument with him. At that point in his life, he never considered anyone else's opinion valid.

Anyway, the day after I hallucinated, Grandma Carol took me to a doctor who put me on Ritalin. As Grandma Carol remembers, it seems the doctor thought the drug might help calm me down. This couldn't have been further from the truth. When I started taking Ritalin, I couldn't get any sleep, so things went from bad to worse. We went back to the doctor who wanted to prescribe something else. I don't remember if it was another drug altogether, or if he wanted to prescribe a sleeping pill to take on top of the Ritalin. At any rate, my mom put her foot down. She said no to the new drug and took me off Ritalin. Then she took me to a Christian Science practitioner. As you know, your grandma was raised in a Christian Science household. When she didn't know where to turn, she went to what she knew.

Lucky for me we went to Elanita Cherry, a Christian Science practitioner, who was awesome. A practitioner is a very sacred position in that tradition. I remember sitting in her warm and inviting office which was in her home. Her office looked out on a courtyard filled with trees. It was an airy, peaceful space where I felt safe. Elanita told me the abuse was not my fault. She taught me that God is love. She also taught me how to visualize being in a protective bubble when Grandpa Lin was mad and abusive.

To this day, because of Elanita, I picture a loving God not a judgmental one. So here's what I think helped to save my life and saved me from further physical abuse: My brother made sure that Grandma Carol stopped the abuse and Elanita taught me that the abuse was not my fault, which I had truly believed. She taught me that I was and am worthy of love. To me, that day with Elanita was a miracle. Somehow, in every inch of my being, in the deepest parts of my soul, I got it. *God is Love.* I am lovable, and I am loved. The abuse was not my fault. I may have come to the realization about not being responsible for causing the abuse with the help of another counselor, but I really, truly believe going to see Elanita was a miracle that caused the shift.

For me, God is Love has been an important thread throughout my life. And I feel the relationship is extremely personal, which may be the reason that I wasn't great at introducing you to organized religions. I've explored many of them and have been dismayed by the various portrayals of a judgmental

God. That portrayal has never made sense to me.

I do remember when you'd come with me during one of the times I explored different religions —our brief stab at finding a good fit for a church. You were a total tomboy and didn't care what you wore as long as you could play kickball in it. You were more into bell-bottoms, t-shirts, and sneakers than belly shirts, frilly skirts, or dresses of any kind. Still, for church, I'd ask you to wear a dress and you'd ask, "If God doesn't care how I look the rest of the week, what makes him care on Sunday?" Looking back I think my idea about dresses was more about the outside appearance for the congregation than how I felt about respectful dress. Normally, I wasn't one to care about appearances so my insistence on dresses must go back to my impressions of judgment in church. Lesson learned.

I'm still working the "love one another" angle. In my opinion, for humans to evolve to where we *could* be, we need to learn to accept and love one another. I'm not there yet. The ones who need that love most are the hardest for me to accept and not judge. I don't need any help learning how to be judgmental. In fact the opposite is true. I work every single day to be less so. I believe religions often control by promoting fear, and I believe fear can often make people more judgmental about what's right and wrong. From my experience, each religion claims to know what God thinks and wants. Following a strict dogma isn't the answer for me. I've always believed the ultimate gift would be for us to just love and support one another. I see God as a universal energy that we really can't capture with our minds, pictures, or words.

About fifteen years ago, I was meeting once a week with a group that explored different faiths which in turn caused us to explore ourselves. One night, the group leader asked us to paint a picture of God's energy. I was stumped. I didn't know of any paper that would be large enough or any paint that would be vibrant enough to capture our universal energy. God and that energy are unbelievably vast to me.

Practicing to forgive

I think that when we're traumatized by our parents we need to get really clear about how we would parent differently. At least that was very true for me. I've read about and seen too many instances where one generation doesn't heal and then harms the next. As a result, I believe it's crucial to take a clear look at ourselves before guiding our kids. Even if our childhoods weren't traumatic, it's important to understand how we operate so we can separate our issues from our child's. As I've said, when we've had a rough time, we'll often overcompensate when raising our children. I know that I did. But, hopefully, lots of introspection while you were growing up helped me to grow as a parent.

When you were first born, your dad and I went to counseling to figure out how to create a good marriage and come together as parents. You see, before you were born, we had the freedom to make spur-of-the-moment plans with each other, on our own, or with our friends. Outside of work, we could pretty much book what we wanted, when we wanted. We also believed that when a couple had a baby, they were just adding one person (an infant) to their lives and schedule, which wouldn't be such a big deal. This concept is hilarious!

After you were born, we needed to rethink our strategies, schedules, and lives. Mary (our counselor) was great at this. She would point out to me that your father could not read my mind and that I needed to ask for what I wanted and needed. I learned to be a clear and consistent communicator. She helped your dad learn how to be clear about his needs as well.

Thank goodness for our time in counseling. It made us better parents and better marriage partners. By the way, it was a big stretch for us to put the expense of counseling into our tight budget but it was worth every cent! We figured out which of our adult priorities were most (or should be most) important. Was it to be counseling, a dinner out, or a new piece of clothing? You know which one we picked. We've used many of Mary's tools over the years. We took our own pasts and did our best to learn from them to make your life a good one, knowing all the while your life would be vastly different from ours. And always will be.

Checking your personal baggage

Some of those tools came in handy when your foster brother moved in. Your dad and I thought that fostering a child with the goal of adoption (foster to adopt) was a good path for us. We thought that we wanted more than one child. We also felt that having one biological child would be enough for us. Plus, there were so many children in need of a good family.

So we decided to become foster parents. The experience still seems surreal. All our intentions were right, but the match and our training were all wrong. If we had it to do over again, we would have requested a younger child. We would have asked a lot more questions about that child's history and what kind of home would have been best for him or her to make sure the child was a good fit for our family and that we were the right fit for the child. I think I would have even requested to have some conversations with their previous foster parents. I'm not sure if this is allowed, but if it isn't it should be.

As I said, your brother was with us for two years. During the first seven years of his life, he'd been moved thirteen times. Because of his background, he generated numerous problems. Due to our lack of training, we were in a hell of a position. Our tenacity caused us to search high and low for solutions for attachment disorder. For two long years we tried to become his "forever" family. We found good counselors and bad, good care providers and bad. I read lots of books—some of which I think were good, some not so good. The book *Parenting with Love and Logic* by Foster W. Cline helped me learn how to discipline your brother. I'm in no way saying that Foster Cline has all the answers, but his parenting style was very helpful with your brother. I learned how to parent logically without going into your brother's emotional swampland.

Cline had stories and examples about natural consequences and how to use them when parenting. One of the stories was about a child who was finding it tough to get ready for the school bus on time. The author's solution for this child was for the parents to adopt a casual attitude. He suggested the parents act as though the child's procrastination were no big deal. Just take the child, the child's clothing, and uneaten breakfast to the bus stop, and have the child finish getting ready there. He also wrote that a forgotten lunch was an opportunity for kids to find out what it feels like to miss a meal. I think the reason this book was so easy for me to relate to was because I don't have a mother earth, "caretaker" personality. That said, I'm a very caring person. There's a distinct difference.

Giving the Love that Heals affected me profoundly. It helped me to examine my own emotional swampland. It was a wakeup call. The book gave us strategies we could use to better parent your brother, and you too.

Your brother was great at pushing buttons, which brought up new stuff of our own that we needed to deal with to heal. As your brother moved through different stages he pushed different buttons, and we needed strategies to deal with him and our own baggage that surfaced. For me, I felt anger I didn't even know I had. Between the counseling that your father and I did when you were first born and reading *Giving the Love that Heals*, I was able to get rid of some of my childhood baggage.

I'd love to give you examples of the interactions that caused me to examine my own issues but I feel these stories are your brother's to tell. Out of respect for him, I'm keeping this part of the letter intentionally vague. That said, I figured out which issues belonged to your brother and which ones belonged to me, and how when parenting him I needed to be emotionally healthy and not get triggered into places of unresolved wounds. To be an effective parent, I needed to remember that I was the adult in the room.

Still, we needed help and the state wasn't willing to give your brother the help he needed that would allow him to stay in our house so the (state) social workers moved him. This was a painful time for our family and I'm not sure that we would have survived it without the tools we had in place, our commitment, and all of those who surrounded us with love and support.

I remember when you were twelve and you spoke at a fundraising tea for foster children. Our recollections of your brother's last day with us were so different. I remember picking him up from school, realizing that intuitively he knew he was leaving. When I walked into his classroom he threw himself at me, wrapped himself around me, and held on as tight as he could. Even though he was nine, I could hold him easily. First, I'm no shrimp—five foot eleven inches, and he was very small for his age. So there we were, clinging to each other, both of us crying. I think when you've been moved as often as he had you get really good at knowing when you're going to be moved again. When we got home from school, the social workers were waiting for him. The minute he spotted them, I saw him emotionally disconnect. This picture still haunts me. I also remember the support from our family and neighbors. And, I remember the tears. Lots and lots of tears.

During your speech, when you spoke about that last day, the memory that stood out in your mind was of trying to hide him among the stuffed animals so he wouldn't have to leave. As painful as that day was, I knew we couldn't safely parent you both.

As I've said, your dad and I each spent time in therapy to work on our issues. Knowing how much it had helped us, when your brother came to live with us we took him for counseling, too. The sessions were pretty intense, so you didn't come with us. After your brother left, we took you to a counselor so that your six year old brain could make sense of those two hard years and you could learn how to move forward.

Thank goodness, you liked your counselor. Janet was amazing. I find it a bit amusing that you liked her so much that you stayed with her after you gained the tools needed, pretending you still needed her help. Smart move on your part. You knew how to get what you needed. Thanks for sharing this tidbit with me years later. I'm glad that your time with her was so useful, and that she made it fun.

The good news was that we all learned from the experience with your foster brother. You saw how much therapy helped you deal with our experience, and you knew how to ask for therapy a few years later when you and your friends needed counseling for something completely different. I'm sure your brother also learned from his therapy. We all learned. We learned about boundaries, loving yourself, and advocating for others as well as yourself. We also learned about respect, responsibility, and consequences.

Advocating

The lessons about how to stand up for yourself were extremely valuable when your fifth grade teacher was charged and sentenced with sexual molestation. Before he started teaching at the elementary school that you attended, he'd worked in another district where the principal and a few teachers complained about him. He charmed and lied his way out of facing charges but he *was* transferred to our district. When he got to your school, no one knew about or spoke about his past. Who knows how long he'd been molesting young girls. When you hit middle school, and one of the current fifth graders at your old school told her parent what he was doing, he was arrested.

At that time, some of your friends (one in particular), came out with their stories of what this teacher had done to them when they'd been at your elementary school. You kids were really confused and in pain. Some of the girls thought his behavior was their fault, or they could have stopped him. Not true. Some of the girls that he chose as victims had been through so much in their short lives. My guess is that seeing their vulnerability enabled him to target them. Pedophiles often present sociopathic and narcissistic tendencies, so they can be extremely charismatic. The young girls had a very hard time sorting out whether the teacher's heinous behavior was inappropriate. After all, they'd been raised to respect their teachers, and this teacher was one of everyone's favorites.

Thank goodness that, even with middle school angst, you were able to be a support person for some of the girls who'd been his victims. And, thankfully, because you knew how much counseling had helped you and our family, you stepped up to ask for counseling for all of you. If you had not learned about how much counseling could help from living with your brother, you might not have been able to advocate for yourself and others. Everyone—his victims, their friends and parents, the community—would have been even more sideswiped by this experience without your help.

Carly, always, always seek help when you need it. There is no shame in needing the help of others. Shame. Now there's a *big* subject. I felt shame when Grandpa Lin abused me, and I believed it was my fault until I was taught otherwise. As I mentioned before, I was blessed to have people who taught me that the abuse was not my fault, that I needed to carry no shame, and that I was worthy of love. As I mentioned, I learned this lesson first from the Christian Science Practitioner who helped me see I was not to blame and, later, another counselor. With their help, I healed and saw myself as lovable, worthy, powerful, and not at all a victim.

Still, as a teenager, I had trouble with self-esteem which is one of the reasons I went to counseling in college. I didn't know who I was. I was looking for acceptance from boys most likely because I felt I'd never had it from my dads. During my childhood and through my late teens I asked my father to talk about his abuse and our relationship. He said that if he went down that road he might never return because of the pain he'd caused me and the pain it would cause him to remember and relive it. I don't think he ever knew how much pain he caused me. By not looking at his actions, because of the pain it might cause him, he was never able to understand and provide the type of parenting that every child deserves. Both my fathers (Grandpa Lin and Grandpa J.) had a grave impact on me during my childhood and as a young woman. One gave me up for adoption, making me feel I was unlovable. The other abused me, which left me feeling unworthy of the love that I knew I deserved. I wanted to have something much, much better.

One more thing, kiddo—first I had to learn to forgive. You will need to learn how to forgive others or your anger will eat away at your core. If forgiveness doesn't work, try detachment. I had to forgive or detach from the scars that my dads left behind so that I could move forward. As you know, one of my favorite sayings is that you can be pitiful or powerful. Choose one because you can't be both. I chose powerful.

Moving

When I was growing up, Grandpa Lin worked for Hughes International Communications Systems, a job which required us to move a few times. By the time I finished high school, I'd lived in eight homes. Moving so much was hard for me. I lost friendships. I moved to places, such as Bainbridge Island, where outsiders in high school were never accepted and finding mentors was difficult.

Fitting in was especially difficult for me because I had dyslexia, which nobody really recognized at the time. I was always in the remedial classes. In elementary school, the teachers and my parents just assumed I wasn't paying attention. By middle school, my teachers wrote me off entirely. I couldn't take a foreign language, because, as they made clear, I couldn't even read and write English.

Though school on Bainbridge was tough for me socially, I found my all-time favorite teacher there. Gail is the first person who understood my learning difference, supported me, and tried to help me as much as she could at the time. There's much more information about dyslexia now. Recently, she asked me to speak to one of her classes about what someone with dyslexia can accomplish. It was such a pleasure to give back.

Still, even though I had an extra hard time adjusting to so many new schools, I think that even without my learning difference, moving would still have been really hard on me. Because of that, I wanted you to live in the same house with the same friends, mentors, and parents for as long as possible. From the time you were born until you left for college, you lived in two homes. The first one was only for four months and, as I write this, we still live in the second. So you grew up in one place, which was super important to me. While we're on the subject of stability, you had something else that I hadn't had that added to your foundation—one terrific father.

My observation is that the father/daughter relationship profoundly impacts a woman for her entire life. We wanted your relationship with your dad to be full—where you two had time for just the two of you. When you were young and I had to travel for work, you and your dad bonded like nobody's business!

I remember one of the business trips I took when you were about two or three. Before I left, I fixed you and your dad healthful dinners so that you'd eat well while I was gone. When I got home, I was so surprised to see that most of the food was still in the fridge. I asked your dad what you two had been eating. He told me you ate chips, bean dip, salsa, and pizza. I couldn't believe it and told him that was no way to feed you. He said, and he was serious, "We ate protein and veggies. What's the problem?" It wasn't the diet I would have chosen. And, okay. He was breaking the no-junk-food rule, but you also had a great time and became closer. From that point forward, I knew that you two would continue to build your own healthy relationship. I even planned a few non-business trips, just to allow for your relationship to grow.

Choices

Choose wisely.

To have or not to have? That's the question you must consciously ask yourself before jumping into the *huge* pool of parenting. When I say *huge,* I don't say it lightly.

Picture the biggest pool you've ever seen, or imagined, or longed for (I know how much you wanted us to put a pool in the side yard), and make it larger—much, much larger! Okay, so picture this. When you take the leap to become a parent, not only are you jumping into this huge pool, but when you jump in—no matter how well you swim—at first, you'll only be able to dog-paddle.

And then, there will be the times you'll need to relax and just float and go with what's happening. You know how I can float in any water? It doesn't matter if it's a pool, the lake, or the ocean? Well the water in this pool takes lots of learning to float. Hopefully, you'll have many good "swim coaches and floating instructors." This is what the decision to become a parent looks like to me.

Parenting—look before you leap

Choosing to become a parent is one of the most important decisions you'll ever make. And being a parent is the biggest job you'll ever take on.

Burned out? Same old routine? Too much hassle? Sorry. You can't quit. You'll work there for your child's entire life. And, can I let you in on a little secret? Before I reported for work, I hauled you around for ten months. I was shocked when the midwife told me that the gestation period of forty weeks is actually closer to nine and a half months than nine. She also said that first children are often late, so it could be ten months. Nine months sounded like a huge time to hand over my uterus, but ten? And guess what? She was right on the money. I carried you for ten months.

There are other options for becoming a parent, each with their own "gestation" period. Your dad and I thought long and hard about ours— adoption, fostering, and an equally important option: choosing not to become a parent at all. This option doesn't get as much good press as it should. In fact, I'd say those who choose this path get bad press. Carly, I encourage you to (along with me) support everyone to make the choice that's best for them.

Ever since I can remember I thought the earth was overpopulated. So much so that even before I met your father I planned to adopt. I didn't think I would marry, and I wanted to impact the life of a child by being a strong female role model. When I was a senior in high school I was voted the biggest women's libber of my class. At that time, where I lived, my beliefs were thought to be completely bizarre. So I didn't even think of marriage as a consideration. Remember, I was a senior in 1978 when some thought women were to be seen and not really heard, when women had just been granted the right to get a credit card or rent an apartment without their husband's signature.

This is going to sound odd but there are still men my age from my high school that think I'm difficult because of my strength and the fact that I kept my maiden name, even in this day and age— 2013. Thank goodness that your generation is more enlightened about equality no matter your gender, race, or sexual orientation. Notice I say "more enlightened." We still have a long way to go.

Then, I met your father and I changed my mind about getting married because of the love we felt for each another. My ideas about how to build a family changed too. Prior to our marriage, your dad and I talked about kids and about the options we'd consider. We wanted to see if we were in sync. Thankfully, we were. Your father and I discussed what was important to each of us. We talked about how many kids we wanted. We both knew that we wanted to be parents to at least one child. The biggest question was whether to have a biological child or to adopt. We discussed the pros and cons of each option.

So if you're not sure whether you want kids or not, think about this. Both options are equally great. When and if you meet someone you think you'd like to partner with, please, please, please don't try to talk them into parenting. If this person has made a sound decision not to parent and you want children, my advice would be look for another partner. It's as simple as that.

Carly, parenting is not for everyone, nor should it be. Many people who've chosen to not have kids have had a positive effect on more kids then they'll ever know. Many parents have had an equally negative effect on their kids. There are so many ways to leave your mark in this world and make it a better place.

Let's say you decide not to parent. You have lots of friends and family to provide examples of what this looks like. Many of these folks have impacted your life in profound ways. Not being a parent and having a full life is a great option. I've heard folks say that being a parent is a selfless act and not having children is a selfish one. I don't buy it. The reverse can be equally true.

I've known many people who think that growing old without children will be lonely. I've seen parents who are lonely in their old age and those without children who are surrounded with light and the love of others as they get older. From what I've witnessed, your fulfillment in life is internal and up to you. I've also heard people speak of their children caring for them when they age. Or providing them with grandchildren. While these are wonderful gifts, from where I stand neither of these tasks are a child's responsibility.

Parenting styles

Your dad and I watched many parents struggle because their styles were so different. They confused their kids who had no solid boundaries, no consistent rules. We made sure we were on the same page and we knew how to provide a united front.

If you decide parenting is for you, and you're going to parent with a partner, it's critical to talk in advance about ways you would parent. I've heard people say, "We got a dog as a test run." For me that doesn't pencil out because, as you know, I haven't always been a good dog trainer. (Look at Abbey! About all I can take credit for is that at least she doesn't fight with other dogs. And, I'm not sure how much of that is genetic disposition.) Despite my shortcomings as a dog trainer, I think you turned out to be an amazing, disciplined, passionate, and strong young woman. Of course I'm prejudiced. Most parents are.

We found one method really useful when defining our parenting methods. Your dad and I looked at how people we knew parented, and then we had private conversations about what we each noticed and how we felt about it. At social gatherings, we'd often witness kids begging for rules (including naps, consistent bedtimes, eating what's on your plate) and boundaries by having a meltdown, throwing themselves on the ground, or kicking their parents.

Driving home, we'd analyze the behavior and try to determine the cause. We'd strategize about how we could avoid, mitigate, or deal with those behaviors if they arose (and they did). We also noticed and talked about positive examples where kids felt safe and secure because they ate nourishing food, were well rested, and knew their parents' expectations. These kids were a pleasure to be around so we wanted to learn how we could implement some of what those parents knew and practiced.

If you decide that observing and discussing parenting styles might work for you, a strong word of caution, don't ever let a parent overhear you talking. If you're not in the parent club, people don't want to hear about how you would handle any child's behavior, especially theirs. And if you *are* in the parent club, many aren't interested in other's ideas, comments, or solutions. For some reason, our parent peers aren't like grandma's parent peers, who truly thought it took a village to raise a child, as do dad and I. This doesn't mean that in those days people overrode other parents' decisions. But, if they saw a child acting out and they felt it was necessary to correct that child, they did so, especially if a child was in their home. If they had a helpful word of advice, they'd share it.

When we were raising you, it was not okay to correct or help with other people's children's behavior. I wish this weren't true, but it was. For me, when we were raising you and someone had a helpful hint to add, I usually listened to see if it was a good fit for us. For example, when we decided to try becoming foster parents, I was going to go all out and try to foster or adopt a sibling group. I'm pretty sure now this wouldn't have worked. Your godfather said, "Try one foster child first to see how it goes." Boy was that sage advice. Thankfully, I listened to Richard and tried fostering one child. I trust your generation of parents will be more open to others in their village.

Your dad and I also discussed our own childhoods, what worked and what didn't. I need you to understand why exploring our childhoods played such a large part in why we took the job of parenting so seriously. When our parents were young, becoming biological parents was the go-to option. It didn't even occur to them to consider other options. I don't even think they thought they had a choice about whether to become parents at all. We knew that when it came to parenthood, we did have options, we had choices to make, and we made them very thoughtfully.

Adopting, giving birth, fostering

For me, before deciding to adopt or carry a biological child, I needed to reflect on all that I saw in the families I knew and had known—families who had biological kids and those who had adopted their kids. I knew this decision would change our lives one way or another. Your dad was clear that he wanted a biological child. I was definitely on the fence. Adding one more person to the planet weighed heavily on my mind. In the end, we decided on a compromise—one biological child and two adopted. One more example, Carly, that things don't always turn out how you plan them. As I'm sure you've noticed, you have no siblings.

Other options include fostering a child or becoming a mentor. Aunts and uncles can develop deep bonds with their nieces and nephews. As can close family friends. Teachers can make a huge impact. And what about those involved in the Big Sister and Big Brother program? I'm sure there are many more opportunities to make a positive impact on children's lives.

What you need to do is search internally and see what fits best for you. Once you've found the answer in your heart about whether or not to have children, don't let external forces influence you. Sure, I'm one-hundred percent for listening to and learning from those around you and I hope you will too. But only keep what you believe in your heart to be true. I've seen varied results when people let outside influences affect their decision about whether or not to parent. Carly, you know people who've said they didn't want to be parents and then they were talked into it. You also know those who've been talked out of parenting. If they were truly coerced, from what I've seen (and there are always exceptions), both seem to long for something different from what they have. My advice would be to search your world for examples, ask lots of questions, and return to the answers in your heart. Think deeply. Give yourself time for introspection. Your realizations can be profound, and they might surprise you.

Speaking of questioning yourself and others, and listening to both, I asked a lot of questions when writing this book. For example, I asked folks around me why they did or did not have children. Here are some of their answers:

Let's look at those again. Did any of them surprise you, because some definitely surprised me.

"I would not have been a good parent."

"We wanted more smart people on the planet to counterbalance those who aren't."

"It is my clock and my time, I just needed to have children."

"It was greed, I wanted a little me."

"Counseling helped me determine motherhood was not for me."

"I wanted to give a child a strong female role model."

"Since I was a child I knew motherhood was my calling."

"I thought that I would be a good parent. I would embrace some of what my parents did, improve on other practices and have fun as a parent making a positive impact on our community."

"I am too selfish to be a parent, my time is too important to me."

"My mother was challenging and I wanted a redo of sorts. I also felt that after marriage, the completion of family involved children. Even now as my life has changed and evolved, I know my choice was right for me."

Just a note, Carly. The woman who said that counseling helped her decide not to become a parent has had a huge positive impact on so many kids. She's a recovery room nurse and has traveled all over the world with Healing the Children, helping kids after surgery. And she and her husband have opened their home to nieces, nephews, and exchange students.

Modeling respect

As you know, I've been a student of humankind most of my life, especially when making important life decisions. I watch people that I greatly respect and regard highly. I see how they live their lives, and I emulate what works for me. I've seen some awesome qualities and examples. I watch, listen, learn, and model.

One of my positive examples took place in college and involved a couple, Bill and Alma, who were my landlords, and their daughter, Cassie. They were a remarkable family. Their marriage and love for one another was inspiring. It was a marriage of equals. Their family was a loving family, with respect for each other. As you know, I don't think anyone is perfect. And I don't think we're expected to be. From what I remember, when they ate dinner, Bill, Alma, and Cassie engaged in stimulating discussions where they'd offer and explore different points of view and come to conclusions, sometimes agreeing to disagree. They didn't make being a couple, parenting, or family life look easy or perfect. Life isn't perfect (at least the way I live it, which can be a bit messy). But they made life look interesting, lively, and fun. And I loved the respect they had for each other.

So dig deep to find questions you might have about parenting, answer them in the best way you know how, and be open to all the doors that may open or shut along the way.

Prenatal testing

Speaking of doors... when I was pregnant, Betty (a woman much older than I was, and the wife of Jack, a man whom I worked with), told me why she felt prenatal testing to check the health of your child made sense. This subject was a super scary subject when I was pregnant. It terrified me, but I went through the testing anyway.

Before she married Jack, Betty gave birth to her daughter, who was born with many birth defects and heath complications. Betty really made me think. She shared her story, telling me how special her daughter was and how much she loved her. Still, she said if she had it to do over again, she never would have brought her daughter into this world. As I write this, I *know* that many could choose to be offended and perhaps outraged, but here is what I know to be true—Betty said that her daughter's condition was something that made her child suffer throughout her twenty short years on the planet and, as much as Betty loved and cherished their time together, she would never have wanted her daughter to bear that much pain.

She said that she didn't think it was a heroic to choose to bring a child into the world to suffer so much. Betty felt it was selfish. If you choose to have prenatal testing, you may want to know in advance what you'll do with the information. As my boss, Jon, says, "You can't unring a bell that has been rung." Making this decision—whether or not to have a child with birth defects and who may suffer as a result—will come with consequences. I make no claim to know the "right or wrong" answer to this question.

Another example was a couple where the wife had a genetic predisposition to a very rare, highly-hereditary form of cancer. They chose to have a child anyway. Their son inherited the disease. When the boy was a teenager, his mother passed away from the same form of cancer he'd inherited. So, he was raised by his father with love. The boy lived twenty-one years (the last six of which were brutal). I still look for the logic in this story. I'm very clear that most of us have a choice but, that said, I'm often confused by the choices that are made. Because of testing, you'll have the ability to choose wisely. And, I know you will. If you choose to have kids, you'll make choices that make sense to you.

And, just so we're super clear, Carly. The decision to have prenatal testing and any choices you might make as a result are up to you and should not be influenced by others.

The other choice that your dad and I made when I was pregnant was that we wanted to be surprised by your gender. So, when we had the testing, we asked the doctor not to tell us whether you were male or female. Your father and I were clear that the only thing that we wanted for you was good health. Nothing else was important to us.

As you've seen over the span of your life, your dad and I have a respectful and equal relationship so we weren't concerned about the gender of our child. A boy or a girl could follow his or her passion. Gender barriers and constructs made no sense to us. I know many people wish for one sex or the other. You've seen families who decide to have another child, hoping they'll get the "right" sex. It's a crap shoot. Look around and notice the families that have two, three, or more of the same gender. And still they're disappointed because they have only boys or girls.

Two final thoughts. When we decided to have only one biological child, some people asked, "What if something tragic should happen to your child?" Clearly, Carly, there would NEVER be a replacement for you as our child. You and every other child on the planet needs to know that you're one of a kind, special in your own right, and irreplaceable. Multiples do not guarantee anything. So to us, tragedy wasn't a solid argument for having more than one biological child.

You've heard me talk about the "bait baby," the "easy" first child, who causes parents to think if they have another, the second child will be easy as well. Again, every kid is different. In my experience (from watching others around me) when the first child is super easy, the second isn't, or possibly the rest aren't. So, even though you turned out to be an easy child, we had no desire or need to test the waters and we stuck with our plan to have one biological child only. You.

I truly believe there's something to my "bait" baby theory, although I have no statistics to back it and many people have had the exact opposite experience. If the first child is tough, maybe the idea of another seems overwhelming. The point is, kids are different. And, yes. I've heard you say that God gives you what you can handle. Clearly, when it came to parenting, he/she went easy on us with you. Thanks be to God and the energy of the universe.

Self-Soothing

OUCH!!!!

Even if we don't say it out loud, OUCH is our inner response to hundreds of irritating things per day—and not just the painful ones. Think about it. "Ouch" is a person's natural response to change. Your newborn may howl when 70-degree air hits his or her 98-degree body. What's familiar is comfortable, Ahhhh, and then BOOM! Something different. Things change.

The natural response is to be surprised, maybe even pissed about it, and possibly to gripe about the inconvenience of change with some yelling. It's a dynamic that will keep happening throughout kids' lives—when they accidentally let go of their balloons, skin their knees, miss a goal on the soccer field, or can't sleep.

Overall, exclaiming out loud is a pretty healthy way to acknowledge surprise, irritation, pain, or frustration. Now I'm going to tell you one of the Top Hardest Things a parent needs to do when their child is learning from their own experience. Hang back. When health and safety aren't at risk, hang back.

Hanging back

Yup, I know. Like any parent, you'll want to race over and exercise your superhero powers to stop the hurt—instantly making it all better with hugs, kisses, gifts, promises, and distractions (like singing the silly song that's so dumb it's just gotta get a laugh). But, here's the deal. The best thing you can do for the child you love so much (and even for your spouse, your friends, and your colleagues) is to let your child have the challenging experience, so that he or she can feel how rewarding it is to sort it all out.

It's really, really, *really* hard to not jump in. But, it's one of the greatest gifts you can give to kids. Hanging back will help them realize that they can confront a challenge and get through it on their own. Maybe it will take some ingenuity for them to figure out how. Maybe the surprise of tripping on the train set will help them to think about where they leave their toys. Maybe the skinned knee will smart for a few minutes. But, isn't it better for kids to know how to recover from these sufferings without the magic of mommy or daddy? They'll be better equipped to deal with adversity if they get this self-confidence early. Please note that I'm not talking about cases where they're in any danger or seriously hurt. Then you *do* have to jump in with your super parent powers.

Here's another thing. Too many parents *think* they know what a child is feeling and initiate their own reactions based on wrong assumptions. Or, maybe they *do* know. The parent-child bond is very deep. But, even though you may feel bonded and telepathically or empathetically connected to your child so that you know exactly what they're feeling, your child is still a separate person having a separate experience. And, that's a good thing.

You need to let your child have his or her own experience or they'll never become self-sufficient. When you were a toddler, Carly, you fell down our front stairs. Even though we could see that you weren't in any danger, your father and I both wanted to race over to comfort you. But, when we'd discussed our parenting style, we talked about what would happen when you fell or faced a non-threatening challenge. So, when you fell, instead of immediately running over we looked at each other intently and reminded each other of our pact. The eye contact helped us to keep our pact. Our silent signal helped stop us from running over to comfort you. It was soooooo hard! We were so scared you were going to cry and feel abandoned and our hearts were breaking.

But we forced ourselves to hold back and monitor your *actual* reactions, not the ones our own panic would have instilled in you. And, wouldn't you know, you got up, brushed off the dust, and felt good about yourself for sorting out the tumble on your own. Imagine if we'd run over and treated you like a hurt baby without even bothering to see what a brave, self-confident person you were? If we'd run over, it would have been about us. We would have been helping to make you a baby who was needy, instead of one who knew how to self-soothe and could grow, learn, and depend on yourself. Of course, we were **tuned in** just like the parents I previously mentioned. We just didn't **butt in**.

Here's another way of looking at why it's important to hold back. My current boss, Jon, suggested that if you watch a child's reaction to his or her fall you'll have the opportunity to see if the parents are raising an independent, capable person, or a person who needs the reaction of others to find their place in life. You know how kids will fall down and look to their parents to see how they're supposed to react? Well, think how that behavior might manifest in adulthood. Those adults might have a hard time understanding how to react to situations. As a result, they might constantly look to others to tell them how to think or feel—perfect victim material. This dependency on others can cause great harm to those adults. "Lots of power being given up," Jon said. "Is this what you want for your child?" I love his analysis.

As I've said, holding back can be really, really hard. One of the toughest parts of being a parent is watching your child suffer. I remember when you were a freshman in high school and left your backpack at a local soccer field. The school year had just started, your schedule was overwhelming, and we were still trying to find our rhythm. You finished your soccer practice, got a ride home, and were all set to start your homework when you discovered your backpack was missing. We drove back to the field, and after searching high and low, we found your pack, but your iPod and math calculator were missing. You were so very sad. There were tears.

Dad and I knew that we'd need to let you replace your missing items on your own. We really wanted to help you by replacing them for you, but we felt the best way for you to learn to take care of your stuff was to earn the money to replace what you'd lost yourself. It was nice that you always had a bit of money put away from birthday and holiday gifts. Your babysitting money also came in handy when you had to replace your iPod and calculator. We sure didn't enjoy teaching you this lesson. Being a parent is a tough job.

As an adult, you're still going to need to comfort yourself, to dust yourself off and keep going, to determine what to do when you've lost something you wanted. Your dad and I sure needed self-soothing techniques to avoid freaking out while we hung back and let you learn to soothe yourself. I think all parents need to know how to soothe themselves during the roller coaster of parenting. To be effective, they need to maintain their equilibrium when their kids are crabby, rebellious, or dismissive as they grow up and pull away.

Most of the time, you shouldn't take your child's upheavals or dismissals personally. If you do, you'll look to your child for affirmation and approval instead of remaining centered and consistent. Look at how many couples become unhealthily enmeshed or co-dependent by relying on the other to build their sense of self. You can see this dynamic in couples, friends, and work relationships. So whether you practice yoga, meditate, take bubble baths, or give yourself pep talks, be sure *you* have good self-soothing strategies to pull you through when the going gets tough.

And when they don't work? Talk to each other. Parents and kids both have ups and downs. A friend told me about how her son coped when he thought she was being crabby. He was pretty sure he hadn't done anything wrong, so instead of blaming himself and slinking away, he'd check his perception. "If you're crabby, just admit it," he'd say to his mom. If she was, she'd fess up and he'd sigh and relax his shoulders.

Now let's take a look at what self-soothing looks like for kids at different stages of childhood.

Birth through age two

Babies cry. It's an automatic response. It's the only way they can communicate that they're hungry, frightened, lonely, or uncomfortable. They might be exercising their lungs, repositioning air, acknowledging discomfort, trying to attract your attention, celebrating their environment . . . who knows? And think about it. Babies are assaulted with an enormous amount of new information every minute. Their learning curve is steep. They're on overload. Who wouldn't cry? But one thing's for sure. If you don't thoughtfully manage your responses to their crying then your baby will figure out that crying means they'll get doting mommy's or daddy's undivided attention, and doting mommy and daddy will go crazy. Crying will become the default activity to keep mommy and daddy on a short leash.

We had help learning this one. Luckily, we had a great, clear-thinking, pragmatic pediatrician when you were born. Dr. Kyle Yasuda took one look at beautiful nine-pound you and figured out that you'd be just fine with daytime feedings and the occasional overnight snack. He encouraged us not to "reward" your sleep disturbances with feedings, because doing so would cause your disturbances to not only continue but also become more frequent. Many parents get into this depleting cycle when it's not necessary (for a smaller baby it might be necessary to feed more at night, but at least have the conversation with your pediatrician about whether it's physically recommended or just a psychological treadmill).

Wisely, Dr. Yasuda told us that if we thought you needed some milk during the night we could give it to you, but we should make sure it wasn't enough to make it worth your while to demand it routinely. We also talked about changing your diaper during the night. He said that unless your diaper was poopy, you could make it through the night for a morning diaper change.

We listened closely to each bout of crying (there weren't very many!). Our responses differed depending on the situation, which we could usually determine by your cry. It was pretty easy to determine what you needed. Until you were four months old, you slept in a bassinet in our bedroom. And in our next home, our bedrooms were next to each other until you were four. As a result of our setting up some intelligent boundaries, you slept well and we slept well. Most importantly, you learned how to soothe your own smaller discomforts (a skill we all need throughout our lives).

And as you grew, you learned how to analyze your problems and ask for help when you couldn't resolve the problem on your own. The important thing here is not to replicate exactly what we did, but to make a personalized set of parameters that are appropriate for your family and your child's specific circumstances, and then stick to them.

So how do you connect at a deep level with your child if you're not jumping up to minister to every whimper? Your wonderful first nanny, Maffe, helped us with this one. She was only nineteen, a single child from Colombia, and her background was rich with extended family, community, and lots of children. She had a natural ease around children. Watching the way she was fully present with you (tickling, making faces, playing games) helped me realize that even while setting firm parameters, you can share incredibly intimate moments of connection with your child. These moments between parent and child are far more meaningful than the more generic "pseudo-soothing" of overreacting to every cry. We'll always be grateful for the help she gave our family and for all she taught us.

During nap time you learned to enjoy and understand that time alone was not a punishment. One of the ways you soothed yourself during nap time was with your binkies (pacifiers). I wonder if you remember having one in your month and one in each hand. You were so in love with your binkies that you'd try to talk with one in your mouth. However, we would insist you remove it before speaking because we couldn't understand you and listening to you talk around it was irritating as hell. The day you gave up your binkies at your dentist's insistence was a very sad day for you. You traded them in for a dolly. The trade didn't work that well. You were off the binkies, but I don't think you ever liked that doll.

In retrospect, I'm not sure that the exchange needed to happen that way. I should have done some soul searching to figure why you were still using the binkies. You know how when we talk about health concerns, that I think that some concerns in Western medicine get covered up with drugs and that essentially we're treating the symptom and not the cause? This practice caused me to think how removing your binky was similar to treating only the symptom. In hindsight, I think I should have searched deeper for why you relied on your binky. You know me, I like get to the bottom of what might be causing the issue to begin with. I'm sorry that I didn't do that with your binkies.

Ages three through five

Most people talk about the "terrible two's," but age three seems to me like a much more difficult stage. It's extra important to keep up the habits of consistency that you initiated during infancy. Three-year-olds are not only bigger, but they're also more mobile, more verbal, and even more desiring of their independence than two-year-olds. Don't assume birthday number three is the end of the rough time.

Tantrums in particular become more intense. You might be increasingly tempted to put an end to them quickly, by any means necessary, even if it means compromising your hard-earned parameters.

Tantrums can be a necessary means for children to release anger and/or frustration, so as a favor to both you and your child, try to figure out how to let these tantrums occur in controlled, safe, (and yes, minimally disruptive) conditions. Tell your child that it's okay to have a tantrum in the privacy of his or her own room, or in a specific "safe chair." Designating a tantrum zone puts parameters on the chaos and helps children understand that they can take care of their own emotional needs with minimal disturbance to others.

When children are feeling calm, teach them different ways to entertain themselves. Children's ability to self-soothe is related to this ability. You can encourage them to entertain themselves by teaching them how to invent their own games. So much can become a game if you look at it playfully. Knowing how to invent games will serve them well during those minutes of meltdown and time-out. The sooner they learn how to engage their brain by entertaining themselves, the more easily they'll be able to engage their minds to shift from anger to serenity, fear to faith, or blame to self-reflection. They'll also be able to stand being in places they might not want to be. Finally, if they can amuse themselves, they'll never be bored. As the famous French author Jules Renard said, "I am never bored; being bored is an insult to one's self."

When you were little, the smallest bug would entertain you for long periods of time. Your stuffed animals, dolls, and books took you to new worlds. And being outside in the fresh air gave you new perspectives of the world when you needed them most.

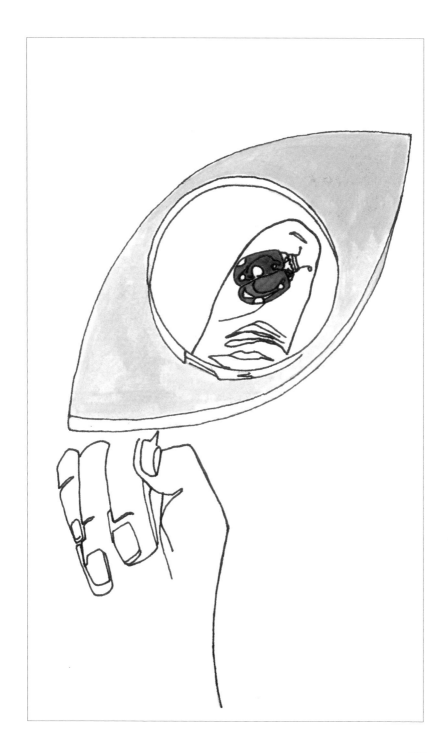

Another strategy to help children self-soothe might be to point out how good it feels when they're at peace. By doing so, you're giving children something positive to shoot for that's within **their** control. You're showing children how to shift how they feel. Since we can't control other people's emotions (and shouldn't try to), it's extremely important to learn to be at peace with **ourselves** throughout our lives. Teaching children that no matter how many times they fall down or miss finding peace, it's worth it to continue to try. It's not how many times you fall, it's how many times you get up that counts. Carly, as you and I both know, we all go through tough times. The outcomes will depend on how we handle them externally and internally.

Finally, when you parent, if you parent, remember not to expect perfection. You may need to readjust your expectations to fit your child's age, stage, and spirit. Recently, I've had a number of folks tell me about their children's learning difficulties and how they've mourned the loss of a "perfect" child. Announcing these feelings of loss to those you don't know well, talking about children who have learning differences as though they're defective, does them a great disservice. There are no perfect kids. And each child is unique, with something special to offer. I feel really strongly about this. I have a learning difficulty, and I don't feel or think that I'm broken. IQ is only one measure of who we are. Try to turn any friction that may arise into learning experiences for both of you. When all else fails, remind yourself of your child's good qualities and be patient for them to re-emerge. They will!

Ages six through ten

Here's another take on the "safe chair." When you were about ten, during dinner one night, you, your dad, and I had a pretty intense "discussion." Okay, it was a huge fight. I can't remember what it was about. But at the peak of the argument, you stood up, left the table, and headed to your room to find the pad of paper where you'd drawn your "safe space" during day camp. Your dad knew nothing about your safe space, and he assumed you were brushing off the entire conflict. Such chaos—you heading for safety, your dad chasing after you, shouting at you to not walk away, and me following him, trying to get his attention to explain that you were going to calm yourself. So there you were, in your room, crying onto your freshly-decorated piece of paper that was supposed to soothe rather than agitate. Thank goodness you didn't give up on comforting yourself. Okay, onward.

While children ages six through ten are developing more and more self-awareness and independence, different challenges start cropping up. Just as you (as a parent) are breathing a sigh of relief that school hours are getting longer and the longer school days are supplying some additional structure (which takes some pressure off you), kids' interpersonal "politics" are getting more complex. Yes, academics are important, but to me, it's even more important to develop the ability to deal positively with unfamiliar environments, social strata, rules (both spoken and unspoken), other parenting styles, schoolyard politics, sports, and so on. Flexibility and self-soothing are important tools for coping with the emotional rigors of this time of life. Parents who understand the psychological makeup of their children can evaluate the demands of a particular situation and work with their kids to help them figure how to navigate this new world while remaining true to themselves.

In grade school, kids need to be okay when the going gets tough. For you Carly, there were times when mean girl behavior popped up, and it was your job to figure out how to handle the situation. I remember when we walked home from school, and we'd talk about your day. You would try to figure out how to maintain certain friendships, how to analyze experiences, and learn different problem-solving strategies. You were always one for figuring things on your own. It was rare for you to want or need your dad or me to help you (defend you) or fight your battles. I think you felt comfortable taking on these challenges because you'd been learning to self-soothe for so long. I know the idea of "so long" seems funny when you think about how young you were, but from your perspective, you'd been learning to self-soothe since birth—one-hundred percent of your lifetime. *But,* young brains have an amazing capacity.

Some self-soothing is learned, but some comes organically as we accumulate experiences that help us understand difficult or traumatic situations.

When you were in the third grade and broke your right wrist on the playground, you cried a lot, and who wouldn't? It must have been terribly painful and scary. When you were in fifth grade and broke your left wrist (again on the playground), you cried much less, which caused the school nurse to assume it wasn't broken. But it was. The reason you cried less was that you'd already been through the experience of a broken wrist and knew that the pain would eventually go away. You knew you'd be fine.

I've always felt that recognizing patterns in one's own experiences is a huge source of comfort. When your child doesn't recognize the similarity between something that happened in the past and again in the present (and with a better outcome), point it out!

Ages eleven through thirteen

You might think that things will get easier during these years, as your child gains maturity and spends more and more time with peers and at school, but the complexity of challenges they face, and the skills demanded of them—both intellectual and emotional—increase exponentially. I remember when I was this age, we moved, and I attended a new school where fitting in was crucial. The challenges facing those who didn't fit in were pretty intense. I never did find a peer group I meshed with. So self-soothing was vital, because bullying and peer pressure (not to mention academic pressure—more demanding in that new school) hit me square in the face. It was a harsh reality. Because of the abusive environment I was raised in, I wasn't good at self-soothing, or maybe I was, but the ways I chose, drinking, partying, and looking to others for approval weren't good choices.

Kids need to have inner resources to draw on when it feels like the world is against them. Each child's challenges will be different, so try to adjust those self-soothing techniques you teach to them accordingly. You experienced several kinds of schools between the ages six and eleven, each of which required different coping skills. You went to a public elementary school, but we didn't think the middle school you were slated for was a good fit. It was extremely overcrowded. And a teacher at another public middle school told me that she wouldn't send her dog to this school, let alone her child.

All, and I mean *all*, the kids in the neighborhood went to private schools, which may have had something to do with why you lobbied hard for going to one. Given the state of the middle school we'd been warned against, we decided that for our family this would be a good move. Even though as parents we had the last word, you always had the opportunity to have a voice. So we chose to tighten our belts, and go with the private school. Like almost any experience, it was a mixed bag, which brings up an important point. There is *no perfect school*, just like there is no perfect parent, lover, job, boss, employee, house, or book.

You're always "buying in" to a particular set of challenges and rewards. Sometimes the challenges themselves can wind up being rewards in disguise, if they help you develop useful capacities that wouldn't have emerged in easier circumstances. Though you missed the diversity of your elementary school (where more than 50 languages were spoken!), learning how to exist and thrive in a privileged private school environment—by remaining true to your own values without getting swept up in the superficial hierarchies—was an invaluable part of your education. Let's just say that all choices have positive and negative aspects. As we found out, for you, this decision had more negative aspects than positive ones.

It was hard to stay centered, no doubt about it, especially when your classmates had so much pressure coming from their own families to outshine each other. Many of your classmates were focused on amassing college resumes, determining who lived in the biggest house, took the best family trips, and had the smartest parents. It probably helped that we de-emphasized these things at home. Your arsenal of self-soothing strategies also helped a lot.

Art was always one of the ways you found peace and centering. You loved art. We've been framing your art since you were a toddler and created your first scribbles on paper and cloth. We still frame your art. In middle school, you pursued your love of art by taking photography. Your teacher saw your potential and your love affair with the camera and really encouraged you. I still think about how happy you were to learn the craft and see the results of your increasing skills. I was so grateful for that class and your amazing teacher, because during those two years, you found your center through photography.

One of the toughest aspects of private school for our family was the large amount of homework you were expected to do each night. You had between two and four hours each evening and every weekend, except for three weekends during different holidays. At home, we always emphasized the work/play balance so having you slog through that amount of homework didn't work for us. We knew that during the evening we needed to have time and space to connect as a family. And weekends were meant for us to enjoy each other. We went to our cabin to ski, sled, and just be. We went to soccer matches, met with friends and family, or just hung out. If your school swallowed up too much of your time, we didn't feel that you'd grow into the woman we knew you could be.

We also knew that we had only a finite amount of time with you in your childhood. That time was precious and would go by quickly. Every child has gifts to share, and some of those gifts don't come in the form of answers to gradable homework assignments. We wanted you to have a childhood in addition to an education, and as a family, we wanted to have more quality time together. We knew you were smart and motivated and could learn what was needed at most any school. So after two years, we agreed you should leave the homework and performance-driven private school. I think we found a pretty good work/school balance after moving on. Just one thing, if you'd been happy and thriving in that school, even though we didn't see our family as a democracy—your opinion definitely held weight, but we had the final say-so—we may have made another decision. We would have found a way to make it work.

Next stop on the middle school journey was an alternative school with only 30 students. This was your third year of middle school. It was a hard transition for you because there were only three girls your age, and they had already formed a bond that was not exactly welcoming to another girl. But, clever girl, you worked around this by finding other friends both inside and outside school. You also connected with the teachers. You found ways to hit your stride and find comfort and success. For example, you decided to head the midyear fundraiser. Boy howdy, did those involved with the fundraiser like your moxie! And you built such great leadership skills. That year, you and I had a lot of driving time together without other kids (there were no carpools), and that time in itself was a gift. We talked about so many things.

One more thing about self-soothing at this age and beyond. Team sports can start becoming a big part of kids' lives. Your dad and I looked at sports performance from different angles, because of our different experiences during childhood. Your dad had had a strong sports background and loved competition. I'd had no involvement with sports and hated competition. And I believe it's vital for parents to keep things in perspective by reminding their children that "it's only a game," and that their personal worth is unrelated to the scoreboard. Many of your teammates' parents gave exactly the opposite message. We watched the result of high-score-equals-worth with your peers, and it was sad to see what was happening to their self-esteem. It's important to learn to lose or fail graciously, without any negative reflection on your own self-worth or lovability.

I remember several games where this lesson wasn't easy. But in the end, I think you figured out how to lose with grace. Look at the upside—a person who is comfortable with failure will be willing to risk more, learn more, and grow more.

Ages fourteen through eighteen

The high school years. Phew. The prospect of independence can be both scary and alluring to kids. They may want to gain some distance from their parents, but they'll still have questions and insecurities. My advice, Carly? Don't try to keep your child dependent on you for advice and input, as though you're the Oracle at Delphi. Resist the temptation to retain one-hundred percent control over your child's malleable mind. Rather, teach your child how to seek a variety of perspectives from appropriate people about an issue, weigh those perspectives, and make thoughtful decisions. Discuss how to change course if your child finds that a decision isn't working. Let your kid know that nobody has all the answers or gets every decision right, and that making good decisions is a skill that can be honed. If you don't push too hard, you'll probably find that yours will be one of the perspectives your child will seek out. Do your very best to never, ever make your child feel like it's necessary to be someone else to gain your love or respect.

When you were in high school you had some teachers who, let's face it, weren't very stimulating. When you'd come home from school and tell me how awful the time in class was, we'd strategize about ways to help you maintain your focus (stay present) in class without hating where you were. We decided you'd try to concentrate on each teacher's good qualities, however subtle. You did your best to stay grounded and derive some value out of even the most lackluster parts of school. Focusing on the positive will also help you in the future with bosses, coworkers, customers, even your own children, if you have them.

Carly, the high school years are a prime time to introduce or deepen the concept and habit of volunteering. I want to remind you of a time in elementary school when you first put your money where your mouth and heart were. Remember when you gave me the $11.37 out of your piggy bank to open up the bank account for our non-profit? I do.

And I also remember all the hours you gave to help that organization grow. Both those acts of kindness paid you back tenfold. At our non-profit, we had to be extremely resourceful. You learned to be the same. You also learned that change is possible, that you could make changes to better yourself as well as the world around you. You learned that many people in the world face challenges so much greater than ours. You learned how lending a helping hand or offering even a small bit of money could make a huge difference. And, you learned what a big undertaking opening a non-profit is.

Helping others—especially by working for a cause kids believe in—offers them an amazing opportunity to learn about themselves and the world around them. Their own problems shrink when focusing on someone else's. Few activities are as effective at soothing teenage self-obsession and instilling a sense of self-worth. If your child has already seen you volunteering, all the better!

Carly, in addition to giving so much of your time to our non-profit, I remember when you initiated walkouts from school for the causes that you believed in, and that you also volunteered at an orphanage. Through your involvement with these causes, you saw those children and parents who had not learned to self-soothe and as a result made bad choices. You saw the results of those choices. You quickly learned the "gifts" received by volunteering. You learned what it looked like to be a capable adult with strong coping strategies.

Being Present

WOW.

I had no idea how to be present for you when you were a newborn. Thank goodness for Maffe. She was a master and taught me a ton. Okay, I had some idea. I mean, clearly, when you hold your infant it's easy to be present. They're right there, in your arms. But many people are too present. They pick up their infants every time they cry. Your dad and I thought that holding you 24/7 would rob you of the space you needed to develop and to become who you are. We wanted you to learn how to self-soothe, and we also knew that we wanted to be present for you. If we held you 24/7, we'd be so wiped out, we couldn't be present for you. At all. By being present, I mean that we needed to show up physically, mentally, and emotionally. We needed to be there for you, heart and soul. And sometimes we needed to pull back. We had to find that balance between being there for you and giving you the room you needed to develop. Looking back, I think we found it. For many this might be a delicate balance. It was for us as well.

Being present for your kid will be the absolute best gift you can give. Better than any holiday gift, birthday surprise, or material object. Kids forget those things. Or, at least those items don't make as deep an impression as quality time spent together.

Being present takes time, energy, and effort. In any relationship, it will pay off in spades.

Think of the times you're with a friend and they're physically there, but that's about it. They're not tuned in. It's such a bummer, right? Or what about when you're around a couple who talk over each other, because they're not really focusing on what the other is saying. They're not really there for each other. Each person just cares about being noticed. These types suck all the energy from others. They need that attention to fill themselves up. I think of them as having their cups half full. Unlike adults, kids don't always know how to fill their cups. While they're learning, they need you to help them. If you're not present with your kids in childhood, they may never learn. They may turn into a person who doesn't know how to be there for themselves or others, one of those people who sucks all the energy from those around them.

When helping kids learn to fill their cups, you want to let them know you have time for them, that they're your highest priority, and they're loved. *But*, at the same time, they're not the center of the universe. Kids might be the center of *their parent's* universe, especially as infants, but they're not the center of *the* universe. WOW. What a balance.

I know that you've met the center-of-the-universe people too, those folks who take up all the air in the room because they have to be the center of attention. Often, they don't listen to anybody else. And many times they can't even put themselves into another person's shoes. They can't understand how another person feels or thinks if it doesn't match how they feel or think. There are many psychological reasons people can be like this, many of them originating in infancy. I think neglect and the resulting inability to self-soothe in a positive manner is one of them. I also think often they were indulged to believe that their time and thoughts are more important than others. See how fine a line this is?

So, here are some of the ways that I think one can be present. *Get rid of your phones, computers, and TV's for a certain portion of time every day.* Carly, when you were growing up, we didn't let you watch TV during the day, and on most school nights —we didn't have the extra time to waste. We spent a lot of time together so being around each other was fairly easy, but I still needed to practice being present. This doesn't mean you never watched TV. We had a few favorite shows we watched. But we seriously limited screen time.

Yep, down time is super hard to do in this day and age. Just this morning, your dad and I took a walk. It was beautiful. This is Seattle, so it was cloudy, but it felt great to be outside. The Douglas fir trees stood tall, and Puget Sound was gray and choppy. We felt really lucky. As we walked, we saw a family coming toward us. They weren't talking to each other. The mom and dad each pushed a jogging stroller, each holding one child. One was an infant, the other a toddler. The toddler was focusing on an iPad. The family wasn't communicating. They didn't even notice the view. Now, I don't know their circumstances. I have no idea if the parents had been up all night with the baby and were too tired to even raise their heads. I don't know if they were too burned out to deal with their little boy who wanted to play with his iPad. I *do* know that it made me really sad to watch them. It made me sad that the little boy was missing out on the beauty around him.

Carly, I know that you're better at being present than I am (my job has often required me to stay close to the phone), so, depending on the type of job you have, it may not be hard for you. However, once you get a career, manage your own living space, and start a family, the schedules tighten, and time seems to get squeezed. So dual-tasking (which some say is impossible) becomes more necessary. Being present for your child can sometimes fall to the wayside.

BUT, don't let it! By being present for your child, your child learns to be present for themselves and others. Carly, you are one of the most present people I know, sometimes to the point of annoying me. For example, since you started high school, there have been times when I've wanted to get in touch with you by phone and can't, because you haven't taken your cell phone with you, or you've taken it and turned it off (or maybe you were screening me!). That said, when you're with us or with your friends, I'm impressed by how rarely you look at your phone for texts, emails, or missed calls. I appreciate your presence.

When you continue to be present (and it takes practice, constantly bringing your mind back from wherever it's wandered), you'll experience life so much more fully. I've heard you describe times where being fully aware has benefited you greatly. For example, when you talk about surfing and how much you love it. I recall your descriptions of being present. You talked about being present to the beauty around you, how much you loved sitting on your board out on the ocean, just you and Mother Nature. At the same time, when you caught a wave, you also had to be present and in the moment to stay on the board.

After helping your child to self-soothe, being present is the second hardest thing that a parent will ever need to do. If you can be present consistently with your child their cup will get filled. Again, no one is perfect. We didn't master being present all the time. Sometimes, because your dad and I were both self-employed, we thought we needed to be available to our customers far too often. We took all their calls, even on the weekend, and sometimes during dinner. In hindsight we should have shifted our goals and priorities.

Oh, did I forget to mention? Consistency is the key to all of my suggestions that make up *The Invisible Parenting Handbook*. Yeah, you know me, that's something else I do—pound a point home. Sorry kiddo, just bear with me. If you take no other suggestions from me about parenting, and learn what you can from others along the way, please, please, please remember to be consistent about following and staying on whatever road you take.

Birth through age two

When you were a baby, I liked things to be extremely neat and tidy. Thank goodness I'm over that. Life is so much easier now. It makes me cringe to think how I was when you were little, because I thought I had to be super mom/career woman/housekeeper/wife, and it was just too much! In those days, I worked from home and hired a nanny to take care of you while I worked. When your nanny and I "changed shifts," and I took over, I thought I should say hello to you, get the day's update from the nanny, say goodbye to her, start dinner, make sure the house was clean, check the answering machine, and on and on. I found out pretty fast that plan wasn't working.

So I came up with a new plan that was much more effective. When Maffe and I changed shifts. I'd get an update, say good bye to her and hello to you, and then after she left, you and I would spend some time together, just the two of us. You only needed five to ten minutes, and then you were happy. Dinner, cleaning, the answering machine? I put them all on hold.

The odd thing was that spending just a little time together made all the difference in our relationship and made the rest of the day go so much smoother. It's the old saying about quality time versus quantity time. The time you and I spent together had to be free of dual-tasking or distractions. By the way, I've heard—and I can't remember where, so I'm not stating this as a fact—that only two-percent of the population can actually, truly multi-task, that when you're performing more than one task at the same time, it's rare to be able to be one-hundred percent present for each. I don't believe much good can come from dual-tasking. Both tasks suffer.

When you were a newborn, I practiced being present by checking on you on a regular basis. Once you were fed, clean, had been held, and were "full" (felt cared for), we'd put you in the baby bouncy chair (the swing that hung from the door frame), or when you were older, your personal favorite—The Walker! We have so many adorable photos of you in that walker, where you're smiling from ear to ear. Now some might say you were too young for a walker, but you were really tall for your age, and we could adjust the height of the walker, so it was perfectly safe.

I remember when you were four months old, and we moved into our current home. We moved our kitchen stuff first, so the living room was still empty. You had a blast running around in your walker in what seemed like a huge room to you. You were laughing, "talking," and so excited by this great big room with all of that space to move. You loved to explore. Of course we were close by and watching you, but you got to explore the new room on your own. Many will say that the devices I mentioned—a bouncy chair and walker—can be dangerous, which they can be, if you don't monitor your child. You'll need to decide what works for you and your family. That said, I would highly encourage you to find a way to be there for your child (as we watched you but let you play), while letting your child be independent.

Side note: You walked very early, before you were a year old. You pretty much went from scooching on your belly to walking. As a result, you had a very brief time when you crawled, which is extremely important for brain development. When you were in middle school, you had an extremely tough time with math. I remember one afternoon you were having trouble with your homework and became so frustrated that you screamed "I HATE MATH" at the top of your lungs. Your best friend's mom, and our neighbor Ann Marie, heard you from across the street, and called to see if you were okay. Anyway, a woman I knew said that your trouble might have been a result of not having crawled enough when you were a baby. So while you were in middle school, I took you to crawling therapy to help balance what you'd missed. Boy, you hated that. Not to mention, I don't think you believe it worked.

We also had times when we would just hang out and be present with each other and the world around us. One of my most vivid and cherished memories is from your first year of life. You and I were out in the front yard. You were about six months old, and we were lying on a blanket looking up through the forty-foot fir tree at the bright, deep-blue autumn sky. The trees were gently swaying. The birds were flying from tree to tree, visiting our bird house, singing, and cawing (all those crows!). I was chattering away about the trees (I've always been a tree hugger), the birds (love those birds and all of their wonderful varieties), and the amazing Seattle sky, as you cooed beside me. *WOW*. What a moment. It doesn't get any better than that.

It's such a gift to be able to retrieve and enjoy moments like this twenty-two years later. When you're present with your child, you'll get many of these moments, and they'll be near and dear to your heart. As difficult to believe as it sounds, you've told me many times that you remember that magical moment. I know as you grew up there were other moments when we were together that you remember as clearly and hold as dear.

Here's a family ritual I know you'll remember. It all started when you were born (although I don't expect you to remember those earliest moments). Your daddy started reading you bedtime stories, which became a cherished ritual. You two would go into your room, and the stories would flow. I loved listening to him read aloud. He was so engaged and enthusiastic, with great inflections. Your dad has said that he read more books to you during your childhood than he's ever read on his own. There were times when he would read the same book for months on end (at least that's what it seemed like to him), but you'd beg and plead to hear the book just one more time and, trooper that he was, you two would start in on another round of *Good Night Moon*, *The Spooky Old Tree,* or *If You Give a Mouse a Cookie.*

We knew that even if you didn't understand the books at first, this special dad/daughter time would create an incredibly important bond between you two. You guys spent this reading time together —often to each other—until middle school (and perhaps beyond). I remember you read each *Harry Potter* book the minute it came out. I believe this reading-bonding time contributed to your passion for books. I love how you still buy children's books as gifts for adults.

Since your dad grew up with sports and is more physical than I am, he took over the rough and tumble activities and sports. You and your dad loved playing air toss, where he'd toss you gently in the air and you'd laugh! You two spent hours wrestling in the living room and kicking a ball around. I was the parent who instigated walks in the neighborhood, parks, and on the beach. The whole family went, and we had great conversations. I love how walking seems to encourage talking and how you still remember those walks and conversations today. You could walk for a long distance as a kid without whining.

Of course we had lots of time together as a family. I was big into family traditions so we always hosted the neighborhood Halloween party, cut down our own Christmas trees, hosted birthday dinners for friends and family, traded off with a neighbor for Easter egg hunts, and held large birthday parties for you in elementary school. You kids had so much fun. I was the mom who never wanted any child to feel left out, so we made sure to invite every one of your classmates. And, because we had a no-gift policy for these parties, they were never a hardship on your classmates. You understood my reasoning. I didn't want people buying or you receiving a lot of stuff made in China by slave labor that you didn't need and would never use. This doesn't mean we didn't exchange gifts with family and friends, but we didn't go overboard.

I love the traditions of celebrations and fellowship. As I write this book in our living room, from time-to-time, I look fondly at the picture of our first outing to the Christmas tree farm. You were around eight months old. We've continued that practice every year since. Such wonderful memories.

Ages three through five

Dinner time! Talk about a great opportunity to be present. I was raised in a home where the dinner table was a major part of our everyday life. Your dad didn't have this same experience. As you know, I love good, healthful food. I love to cook it. I love to share it. And, above all else, I love to eat it. So we made dinner time a top priority. As long as I can remember, I've shared my passion for food with you. Heck, you went to your first restaurant when you were nine days old.

Our family tradition of having dinner together really helped us to be present with each other. One of your dad's highest priorities was to have real conversations, which he hadn't had growing up. His family confused conversation with confrontation. In our new household we had conversations, lots and lots of conversations. I think he got more conversation than he bargained for! We'd sit around the table and eat dinner, chatting and discussing each other's day. We'd sit with friends and family, or just the three of us (or the four of us during the two years your foster brother was with our family).

Your brother initiated one tradition that we practice to this day. He learned it at one of his foster homes. That tradition is holding hands before each meal and going around the table, each person giving thanks for the highlight of their day. I'll tell you what, some days it's really important to try and find that very small kernel to be thankful for. Every time we sit down to dinner—whether it's just the three of us or we're eating with friends or loved ones—I think of your brother as we give thanks.

We're all somewhat familiar with the statistics about how families that eat together bond more closely and that the kids are generally less prone to alcohol and drug abuse. I didn't start this tradition with these statistics in mind. I started the dinners because I loved the tradition and thought it was important. I definitely believe these dinners helped us become closer as a family and helped you to learn the value of being grateful for these delicious, nutritious meals, and to understand that not everyone is so lucky.

After dinner we'd play games. We had some great collaborative games. You know me, always trying to take the competition out of life. So we found Family Pastime Co-operative Games. We spent hours playing Snowstorm, Secret Door, and Grandma's House. We sure enjoyed those games where we worked together to win. It's funny how kids who aren't raised on these non-competitive games don't really see the point of playing them. I still don't think your dad gets it but, you've gotta hand it to him, he spent hours at the table with us playing those non-competitive board games.

We played outside in the neighborhood throughout your childhood. You thought it was great fun, and I enjoyed it too. I also felt it was necessary. After I finished work, or on weekends, we spent hours with many families on our cul-de-sac. We'd all set up safety cones at the end of the street to caution the few cars that drove by, and talk while you kids rode your Big Wheels and tricycles and played in the street and on the driveways. You all had a blast. I know that my being there and paying attention reinforced safety for those kids that needed a reminder to be mindful of the younger children. It helped them think about how they played, taking care not to run into the younger kids or over them (it happened) with their larger faster vehicles. This is not to say that kids don't need to work things out among themselves, but when it came to health or safety, I was always ready to give a stern warning.

Reminding older kids of safety issues when they're playing with younger ones goes back to my childhood. When I was about nine or ten years old, our family lived in California for a brief time, and we had a swimming pool. I remember the neighborhood boys holding my best friend and me under water until it was unsafe. I felt helpless and scared. They thought it was funny. I don't think they were trying to hurt us, but they were just too rough.

When you were growing up, with adults present and making sure the play was safe, you came to love the rough and tough play of the older neighborhood boys. I was fine with letting you get used to that. I just wanted to make sure that when you were too little to defend yourself, the older kids were mindful that they needed to go easy, and you didn't have to experience the horrible feeling of being unsafe that I had.

Here's an example of how important it is to be present for kids and how it truly takes a village. You'll love this example, because once again, it shows my parenting was far from perfect. One Saturday, when you were about seven, your dad was at work, and you were outside riding your scooter, playing with the neighborhood kids. You fell hard on the gravel and *really* skinned your knee. Your jeans weren't ripped, but there was a fair amount of blood, enough so that your pants stuck to your knee.

You knew how awful I was (and still am) with

injuries. I get really queasy when someone describes a medical procedure. Knowing this, after you fell, you just thought you'd be fine, decided not to come to me, and continued to play. Hours later, when your dad came home, you were still playing with all the kids. He noticed the blood on your jeans and asked you what had happened, so you told him and showed him your knee. Being the calm and pragmatic person that he is, he took one look and off to the doctor you went. You needed stitches.

That night at dinner, we made a new rule as a family. No matter how much you hated to upset me with blood, if you were hurt, you had to tell me immediately. Then, I'd figure out if we needed help. Thankfully for us, our neighbor across the street, your best friend's mom, was perfect with injuries. From that point on, "Doctor" Ann Marie was there for us—the go-to practitioner. We were so lucky to find such a great solution right across the street!

Ages six through ten

When you were in elementary school, there was a time of day that I considered our "bestest" time of day with each other. I know from a note that you wrote in grade school that it meant a lot to you too.

Here's part of your note.

My mom is special because she lisens to everything I say. She is nice to my friends so they want to come back. Most of all shes special because shes my mom. I like it when my moms rides bikes with me but the most importent thing she dose with me is walk me to school every day.

Now I know it may not be possible to walk kids to school or to their bus stop every day. Work schedules can get in the way. But carving out time to walk can be important because there are no distractions. You're facing the same direction and you can either share conversation or walk in companionable silence. Carving out this kind of time allows for you to hear more about your child's life. Or, if you drive to school, being in the car together can also work for you, as long as you keep the radio, phones, games, iPods off and the adult conversation to a minimum (if another adult is in the car).

I had the luxury of having a flexible job that enabled me to take time off for field trips. Participating in these trips gave me an opportunity to get to know your teachers and classmates and become familiar with school dynamics. By the time you were in second grade my reputation had taken hold among the teachers. They knew they could count on my help with the more unruly kids and, typically, they made me responsible for six or seven of the tough or energetic boys. Before we'd leave the school, I'd have a serious talk with the boys about expectations and consequences. Our understanding was if they did something that wasn't allowed, they'd get the honor of holding my hand for the rest of the trip. I believe this only happened a couple times before word spread about the rules I set down. After that, we all enjoyed fun, safe trips. It was lucky for the two of us that you got over thinking my behavior was embarrassing because, let's face it, my behavior wasn't going to change. You know how I feel about kids needing boundaries.

Your dad's schedule was not as flexible as mine, but he was present at other activities. He was an assistant soccer coach for your community league soccer team, he attended school concerts and award ceremonies, and he took days off when a school event was really important to all of us.

When you first started playing soccer, you loved it! You wanted to play soccer in the Olympics, to be the next Mia Hamm. My take on sports was that they could be a priority without consuming your life. Many times I'd watch kids in select soccer (the teams consisting of kids who were considered to be extremely strong players) and the impact it had on their families. Select soccer involved an insane amount of practice, games, and travel. From my perspective, for those families involved, it seemed as though their family time and their lives were eaten up by the heavy commitments the program demanded.

I know that for many families, having their kids live and breathe sports works. To them it's a sound decision, but for our family, it wasn't. I wanted our family dinners to continue and to preserve all the goodness that came from that time together. I knew if soccer continued to be your love, you'd beg and plead to join and play select soccer year after year, and we would have probably figured out a way to make it work. Thank goodness soccer was not your only love. You found many more things that were of interest.

Does this mean that you couldn't have been a fabulous soccer player? Nope! It just meant that you (and our family) took a different road. At your height (you weren't your full six-foot-four yet, but you were really tall for your age), quite frankly, you most likely would have been a goalie. And OMG, that would have made me nervous as all get out. Not that my nerves should have stopped you, but I think by not narrowing in on one thing you've found so many different paths to follow, so many things to explore, and—as a result—have discovered so much that was pretty dang interesting for you.

Ages eleven through thirteen

Oh my. Angsty adolescence. This is a critical (and often the most unpleasant) time to find places to be present. I think when kids start to push away, they need parents more than ever. As I've said, being around adolescents is not always a picnic. Sometimes, you want to head for the hills and leave your kids and their hormones behind. But, during this stage, you've got to be strong because they need to have something to push against, something that's solid. They need your strong boundaries while they're testing their own. They need to know you'll be there when they need a break from pushing away.

Carly, I remember during this stage you could get moody. You'd talk to me the same way you would joke with your friends, which can be a very disrespectful way to talk to a parent. We used to talk about it. I've spoken with other parents who talk about how when their kids went through puberty, they'd forget their parents weren't part of the gang, and get pretty rude. I wasn't going to put up with the way you talked back or your angsty attitude. Still, as hard as it often was, I strongly felt I needed to be present for you.

The place I could be present the most was the carpool. In my car, there was no getting around my presence. In that wonderful world of carpooling, I got to hear conversations that I might not have heard otherwise. One really stuck with me. It was during your first year of middle school when you were attending a private school we both felt was more elitist than many. Let's see if you remember this one. It was the morning carpool. We were driving to school, and the first thing one of the kids said was that she wished her father were more important. I asked what she meant by "more important." She said, and I'm paraphrasing, "Many of the fathers at this school are more well-known and/or famous in the community, like, for example, the head of Starbucks."

Yikes! Was this a shocker—Importance and fame being this closely connected?! I mean, Mother Teresa had been famous but poor. Wasn't she important? The janitor at the school who provided such a clean, healthful environment for the kids. Wasn't he important? I would love to know your recollection of this event, if you even remember it. As this young girl spoke about the importance of fame and money, I could feel my temperature rising and thought it best to ask a few more questions, so that I could find out where she was coming from and learn more. But the more she talked, the more I realized I wasn't ready to have that discussion.

I knew if I took the time to cool down and think about what she'd said, and then express my feelings, I could help you and maybe her consider a different perspective. Two days later, in the carpool, I was able to ask more questions and provide you guys with some food for thought. The questions that I asked her had the same theme, that we are all equally important, that every person in our world— rich, poor, known, or unknown—has equal worth.

I spoke a bit about people who've done very important work and no one knows their names, how many people had given great amounts of money and chosen to remain anonymous. I provided several other examples to back up my truth. I'm not sure what the rest of the kids in the carpool felt about this conversation, but I remember thinking that at least it helped them see different perspectives. I often think about all the conversations that you and I would have never had, if I hadn't made sure to participate and pay attention.

When you were eight, you and your dad started the tradition of your father-daughter camping trips. To this day, whenever you come home during the summer, you and your dad still make time to go. I think the times of being together while you planned, gathered your gear, and took the actual trip will always be a high point of your lives, and you'll continue to take these trips for years to come.

When you were in middle school, I think taking these trips allowed you and your dad to be together as your body changed, a time during which many dads can have a hard time knowing how to relate to their daughters. Your dad did say that sometimes it was weird for him to be around as you physically changed, and I told him how important it was for him to maintain a close relationship with you. I think by being present during those years, he helped give you the self-confidence to become a strong, self-assured young woman.

Again, all families are different. I'm just saying this was our experience. I do think it's extremely important during these times for a girl to feel comfortable with who she's becoming and not be rejected because others feel awkward about her changing.

Ages fourteen through eighteen

High school already?! This can't be. And, the pushing away from your parents continued, yet you were very gentle about it. Thank you.

High school is such an important time to be available and present. During your early high school years, before you and your friends started driving, carpooling became even better. By this time, I'd rescinded my no radio rule, but I had my reasons. I'd turn on the radio softly and pretend not to listen to your conversations. I became involved in the conversation only when absolutely necessary. If you weren't discussing a health or safety issue, I kept quiet, if I could—never easy for me. If something concerned me, I'd ask you about the conversation later, when we were alone. I did my best to give you autonomy in some areas of high school and to make my presence known in others.

In my opinion, football games are a great place for parents to participate. As you know I don't give a rip about sports, but I'm happy to cheer the kids on to victory when I know who they are. Your school's games were fun. The coach was wonderful and, as a result, the team did really well. Coaching is such a difficult job, but when it's done well it's amazing to see how it affects the kids—both those playing and those watching.

I loved supporting the school teams—football, basketball, soccer. And I loved supporting the teams on which you played. I went to as many of those events as possible. I helped with soccer and basketball. I watched track and volleyball. I wanted to go to your dances, too . . . kidding . . . but I did have fun teasing you about attending them as a chaperone to see all that went on. You were mortified!

We left your grades to you. We never tracked your performance by looking at scores posted on the school website. It would have felt a bit like stalking. Besides, we wanted you to take responsibility for your grades. I've heard many comments about the effect grades can have on the parent-child relationship. The kids can feel so much pressure that they just rebel or give up.

My advice to you, Carly, would be to have lots of conversations about this with your kid all along the way, letting him or her know your expectations. We were there when your report cards came. We checked your grades. We discussed any areas where you might need help and found a tutor, if necessary. We took an interest in your school work but knew that ultimately it was all on you.

You knew our expectations about your grades. If you were behaving as though your school work wasn't important, maybe placing a higher priority on your social life so that you didn't turn in your homework and your grades were failing, you knew there would be consequences. Our thanks to your third grade teacher, Mr. Langston, who made it clear that school was your job, not ours. He told us that we'd already completed our education, and you needed to be trusted to attend to and complete yours.

One of the aspects I loved about those years was having our home filled with your friends. They were always so welcome. I also know you think you didn't get enough space when you were in high school. I'm talking specifically about the house rule on regarding boys in your room. If you had boys in your bedroom, you had to keep the door open. ALWAYS. I still stand by that being a great rule for middle and high school ages.

Open door rule aside, I gave you and your friends space. But I was also there if any of you needed help, a mentor, or an honest and open conversation. You know I'm always honest and open, many times to a fault. I knew that my honesty with all of you would foster trust during these years. I always knew that I was your mom, so I needed to be your parent, not your friend. When you needed a supportive adult who wasn't a parent, I knew that you'd find one through neighbors and friends or family. I'm thankful for those in the village who surrounded you and were there for you during those years.

Boundaries, Rules, and Manners

NO!

"Because I said so." "Give me some time to think about it." "Please chew with your mouth closed." "Slow down when you eat." "Those are the rules. They came from *The Invisible Parenting Handbook*. When you become a parent you'll get a copy." "Let me check with your dad." And your personal favorite, "Looks like you're hungry or tired." Boy, you hated that one. Mostly because you heard that sentence a lot, and you actually were hungry or tired, but you hated me calling you on it. You'd get really angry. "I am NOT hungry or tired."

You also heard, "Of course you can." "We're so pleased that you made that decision." "Great job." "We know that you want that, how do you think you can make that happen?" "You're amazing." "We love you." "We're so pleased for you." We made these statements year after year while you were growing up. They were our standards when you needed a boundary, or were forgetting your manners, or when we wanted to encourage you.

You'll notice that I didn't say, "We're so proud of you." We intentionally did not say we were proud of you. I don't take pride in you or others or in the actions of others. I don't own you, and you don't own me. The quote by Kahlil Gibran in the front of the book captures my feelings perfectly. Children are separate individuals, not belongings. I know that my identity is not yours and your identity is not mine. I also have trouble with the entire idea of pride. Maybe that's because so many people say "I'm proud of you," when the first definition listed in the dictionary talk of pride as being a feeling people have for themselves and not others.

The Merriam-Webster Dictionary (consulted in November, 2013) contains a definition of pride specifically for kids.

Too high an opinion of one's own ability or worth : a feeling of being better than others

Reasonable and justifiable sense of one's own worth: "http://www.wordcentral.com/apps/apache/docs/wordcentral.com/cgi-bin/student?book=Student&va=self-respect"

A sense of pleasure that comes from some act or possession

Something of which one is proud <our pride and joy>

I take huge issue with definitions 1, 3, and 4— the majority of the definitions. These definitions are the most often used.

I think that many of my parent's peers felt

defined by their children's success. Your identity is yours. Our job was to help you find who you were and what you stood for *and* give you boundaries to bump up against while you searched. Therefore, we were not you, and you were not us. We were your parents.

There is something about our parent peers that has confounded me for many, many years. I think it may have to do with why boundaries, rules, and manners are often moved or disregarded. From what I've witnessed, children need role models and boundaries. When parents don't put themselves in charge and set limits, kids become confused about their roles and that of their parents. This happens in two-parent families as well as single-parent families. When you were young, about ten, your dad and I watched many of our parent peers change their parent-child dynamic to that of friend-child, becoming buddies. The results were grim. There's even a new word for this type of parenting— peerenting.

You most likely remember my asking or telling you to make good choices. I talked about choices a lot as you were growing up. Many times, we talked about making good choices about boundaries and rules. For example, we discussed the need to be respectful to your elders, even when it was hard. I remember the first time we heard the expression "Make good choices." I think it was either toward the end of elementary school or the beginning of middle school. We were watching a favorite TV show. The mom in this show used to say to her daughter, "Make good choices." Ironically, the daughter always seemed to be much better at making good choices than the mom. The mom had been in high school when she'd had her daughter. They'd practically raised each other, so the parent-child roles were blurred—an intentional point, critical to the plot. It's important to make sure that as a parent, your good choices are based on your role as parent and not as a friend.

As you grew up, you understood the importance of having those boundaries to bump up against. They made you feel safe and loved. You also knew that if you did something that you were asked not to do, there would be a consequence. I think boundaries get a bad rap because they're hard to enforce, and being consistent about enforcing them can wear a parent down. Because I was a working mom, I found it easier to be consistent. The fact that I only needed to be able to be strong and unwavering as a parent for seven–ten hours of the workday instead of twelve–fifteen made a huge difference for me. It was also easier for me to remain consistent because your dad and I were on the same page.

When your dad and I grew up, the boundaries were clearly defined. We were taught manners and reminded to use them. If we broke the rules, there were consequences. We also learned the rewards of listening to our parents (okay, not always easy) and showing respect to others. Because we were raised with this model, it was easy for your dad and me to see how natural consequences worked. For example, if we didn't want what was for dinner, fine. We went hungry. If we refused to wear our coats to school, fine. We got cold.

I remember when I was in elementary school, our family was best friends with our next door neighbors. If Mrs. McKenna told me to do something, I listened up and did what was asked. I never would've dreamed of disrespecting her, because I was clear about the consequences. And, she never would've dreamed of not punishing me or ratting me out to my parents. Today, the perception is that our parents were far too harsh, abusive, or over the top, and in many cases this was true. But, for the most part growing up, we knew where we stood and what the expectations were.

Obviously, we were brought up long before building self-esteem was considered of premier importance for kids. Don't misunderstand. I think it is important. I just think we went overboard by presenting a non-competitive view of the world. As I've said, I'm not big on competition. Though I agreed with the non-competitive atmosphere of kids' sports, I didn't agree with getting a trophy just for joining the team or showing up. We were brought up before there were graduations from fifth and eighth grades, and long before your identity was keenly tied to how much better you did than the kids next to you.

It was a conundrum. There was a greater emphasis on being non-competitive, but competition was fiercer than ever. Neither your dad's nor my parents ever compared us with others. My parents always said, "I don't care what she has or what her parents are doing. This is about you and our rules for you."

Today, it seems that the motto is "All for one and one for me." Sure there are contributing factors —the population has doubled and big business has a much stronger hold on political leaders. People are frightened, overwhelmed, and they've lost the belief that one small effort on their part can effect change. But I wish we could return to those days when competition wasn't so fierce, when there wasn't such a driving need to compare yourself or your children to others. Having an individual identity gives a person so much more freedom.

Birth through age two

I found that the simple words were the best ones to teach first. Your dad and I knew that we wanted you to know what "NO" meant from the get-go. I know that some parents don't like that word. But, we knew saying "No" would come in handy if you were ever distracted while putting yourself in harm's way. We could get your attention with a firm "No," and stop you in your tracks. Maybe even save your life, if need be. You were a busy and active child, so "No" was helpful in many instances. It will be unbelievably hard to say "No" a thousand times a day, but you need to make sure you say it anyway. I know I've said this before, but I feel it's important to say it again and again—consistency is the key. And, just for the record, you also learned the words "Yes" and "Maybe."

Kids will parrot your words, which can be frustrating at times. Because you had learned the word "No," when you were a little older, there were times when you used it with us and we would often overrule your "No." As I've said, our home was never a democracy. That is not to say that you couldn't and shouldn't have your say, opinion, or objection. It's just that dad and I had the last word.

Sometimes we listened to your "No." If you were saying "No" to giving someone a hug or to them hugging you, you were always listened to and allowed to decide. If you were saying "No" to a meal, a health and safety issue, or a nap, we usually overruled your objections.

But, we did listen. We wanted you to feel heard. I think active listening plays a key part when your child weighs in. You need to really hear what your child is saying. Ask questions when you're unclear and, later on, listen between the lines. We also felt it was important for you to communicate clearly and effectively. Part of that was learning to think carefully about what you were saying and to back up your points with thoughtful reasoning. Still, we had the final say.

There are rules and codes of conduct in any society, and our home was just a micro-society. When you were an infant, our main rules were that naps were necessary, food and nutrition were a must, and manners such as saying "please" and "thank you" were very important. Lucky for us, you were verbal from a very young age (from what I've seen, girls pick up language more quickly than boys), so communicating to you the need to say "please" and "thank you" was fairly easy for us. And, it was easy for you to use the words with us and with others.

When you were little, the rule about taking naps made all of our lives so much better! So did making sure that you had enough sleep at night. You had a set bedtime for most of your childhood, until you were about sixteen, I think. We were not so rigid that you had to have a nap at the same time every day for the exact same length of time. For example, we were more flexible when it was the weekend or a holiday break. We just made sure that there was time and space for you to get rest every day. If you were out of sorts, it normally had something to do with hunger or a lack of sleep.

Here's a story for you. One day when I was at a local garden nursery, I saw a woman with twin toddlers. She was looking at plants and shopping while trying to bribe the twins to "be good" by promising them a fun activity at the end of the shopping trip. One of the twins was melting down. In-between the tears, he was saying how tired he was. The other twin simply looked on. The woman continued to say that there would be no fun activity for either child if this behavior continued. I really wanted to go up to this woman and give her my two-cents. I wanted to ask her why she felt it was effective to offer a reward to a child who was too exhausted to enjoy it. I also wanted to know why she wasn't taking her kid home to take a nap. As I see it, providing rewards (not bribes) for good behavior is great, but this woman needed to listen to her son. Really listen. He was very clearly explaining his need to take a nap.

Another rule that you learned quickly was not to waste or play with food. Because of my love of food, the cost of good food, and the scarcity of good food from which so many suffer, we had a zero-tolerance policy when it came to your being disrespectful about the food you were served. Once you moved from breast milk to organic baby food, we began working to honor our respect for food. When feeding you, we took your spoon and gently scooped up the food that landed on your face, food that hadn't quite made it to your mouth, and fed it to you, so it wasn't wasted. We also didn't encourage you when you tried to play with your food or spit it out. When you'd spit out your food or stick your tongue between your lips to blow a raspberry (with the spoon in your mouth!), and then look at us for a reaction, we didn't give you one. We didn't want to encourage your behavior.

We taught you and expected from you age-appropriate manners. When you were younger than two, you weren't allowed to scream in a restaurant or most any other place. It's a huge disruption to people frequenting those places, and we did not want to negatively affect their experience (and it hurt my ears!). You weren't allowed to run up and down the aisles in public places—restaurants, supermarkets, department stores. In nice stores, we had a strict no-hands policy. In people's homes, you respected their belongings. You didn't pick up their things, you didn't run from room to room, you didn't open drawers, and you never jumped on their furniture. Do you see a pattern? You were starting to learn to be a responsible member of our society early in your infancy.

Ages three through five

Age three was tough. You didn't like boundaries. You pushed every button you could find. You tested every limit. You were strong-willed and wanted things your way. And, because you were highly verbal, you were clear about how you wanted things to be. So I stepped up my game and got really clear about how I needed things to be. As a result, you threw some amazing tantrums. Thank goodness you had a bedroom where you could cool off. We also used time-outs for both of us. Sometimes I needed my time-outs so that I could calm down and gain perspective about who was the adult in the room. I know it may sound funny that I had to remember who was in charge, but believe you me, there were times that it wasn't funny at all. Once we'd established the new boundaries, everything fell into place. You felt safe, and you knew you could trust what we said and depend on us to follow through.

Another rule you learned from your earliest years was how to enter a conversation. Interrupting to ask a question about something that had nothing to do with what the conversation was about was not acceptable or encouraged. If you were part of the conversation, well that was a different matter altogether. To clarify, let's say I was talking with a neighbor about something important to us and you wanted to go outside and join the other kids playing across the street. Of course you would need to interrupt. You just needed to do it politely. You would need to wait for a pause in the conversation, and say "Excuse me, please," and then ask the question.

On the other hand, if you were included in the conversation, what might look like an interruption to some—speaking up with your opinion while someone else might be speaking—was perfectly fine.

Here's how I feel about that kind of conversation and conversations in general—no one owns them. They're alive (lively), dynamic, a stimulating exchange of ideas. Monologue and conversation are two different things. A conversation may take many twists and turns. Often when talking with each other, I feel that an important point can get lost if it's not captured and shared, so I want to make sure that doesn't happen. That's why I think of conversations as being alive. I know many who will differ with my viewpoint, but I'm a firm believer in speaking up and being heard.

Okay, so here is one on my major pet peeves about conversations. Say you're on the phone with a friend who has children. One of their kids keeps whining because they want their parent's attention. Instead of telling their child that he or she needs to wait until the parent is off the phone, the parent rewards the child by telling you that they need to go. Before you were born, I experienced my friends abruptly ending our conversations on several occasions. The kid might whine, or my friend would simultaneously hold a conversation with me and her child, so that often I didn't know who she was speaking to. Or the parent kept interrupting our conversation to scream at her child. I was *really* irritated. So when you came along, we had a hard and fast rule that unless you needed to go to the emergency room or the house was burning down, phone interruptions were never acceptable. Thank goodness you were a quick study in this area.

Next rule of critical importance to me and your father was that hitting, biting, or hurting others, including animals, was not acceptable. I'm grateful that you weren't much of a hitter. And that when you were an infant, Maffe helped you learn how to be gentle with our dog and cat. If you hit or kicked, you got a strong talking to and a time out. When you went through your biting stage, and you bit us, we bit you back (not hard). You didn't like it, so that habit didn't last long!

Ages six through ten

At this stage, you learned about our family's view of lying. One of our neighbors helped teach you this lesson. I think the neighbor kids and you were playing a game of hide-and-seek and you broke a piece of yard art in the neighbor's yard and then blamed it on another neighbor kid. Boy howdy, did we have a serious talk about lying. And, you can bet there were consequences. You had to apologize to the neighbor and do chores to earn money to replace the object. You also apologized to the girl whom you blamed. Carly, most of the behaviors listed in this chapter are natural for kids. It's how you deal with them that will make all the difference in the world as your child grows up.

I have a few stories about when the folks around us helped us to find ways to clarify the boundaries. The first was when my former boss Linda was in town and visiting our home. She noticed that one of the neighborhood kids was hitting other children while playing in our yard. She asked what I was planning to do about it. I can't believe I actually hesitated to step in, but I did. I was torn. I told her that many of the parents I knew wouldn't react well if anyone scolded their children, and this child's parent had given me hell when I'd disciplined her child before, including when he ran over you with his Big Wheel. My boss said that this seemed like nonsense, especially if this inappropriate behavior was happening in our yard. She said that it was my responsibility to help this kid learn the limits. I explained that this particular parent had explicitly told me she did not like others correcting her child. So Linda strongly suggested a solution.

Here's how her suggestion played out. I explained to the child that hitting was not allowed on our property and if they hit again there would be a one week time-out from our house and yard. Almost immediately the same kid hit one of the other kids playing on the grass. I love how kids need to test those boundaries. I brought the child inside to explain how I would miss him over the next week, and how I looked forward to seeing him when the time-out was up. Low and behold, this kid never hit anyone in our yard again (that I know of).

I totally agree with what Wayne Dyer says on his DVD *Change Your Thoughts, Change Your Life: Living the Wisdom of the Tao.* He cautions against being an overly involved parent by solving or resolving your children's every little quibble. I think there's a difference between parents resolving kids' issues and making clear, immovable boundaries about safety.

Another tip I learned was from a man on an airplane. I was on a business trip, and the passenger next to me and I were talking about parenting strategies. I mentioned that the night before I left on my trips and the night I returned, you often liked to sleep in our bed with us. I said that our bed was getting too small, and I wanted to shift your habit. He suggested that I should tell you that it was fine to sleep in our room on those occasions, but you would need to do it on the carpeted floor. This boundary was so helpful! I've often found some of my best parenting strategies from parents I didn't know in places I didn't expect.

One last rule comes to mind. We started to give you chores. The chores that you had when you were little could be as simple as helping with dinner. The salad spinner was a favorite. You also had to pick up after yourself. After playing with a game, puzzle, or art project it was your responsibility to clean up.

Your bedroom was a different story. It was somewhere in this age range that instead of nagging you about cleaning your room, I'd just shut your door, so I didn't have to look at the mess. You weren't allowed to have food or beverages in your room, so it was never too disgusting in there. After the piles got to be too much, you'd clean your room on your own. Or sometimes, when the mess in your room overwhelmed you, you'd stay out as much as possible, and move homework and art projects into other areas of the house. You knew you had to keep those areas clean and tidy. You had to pick up your homework and projects each day when you finished. It was a pain, and it never took you long to realize that cleaning your room would help you to feel better about your life. We felt this strategy was a great way to help you figure out how a tidy space makes it easier to find things and get your work done.

Ages eleven through thirteen

At around this age you learned how to shake an adult's hand while looking them in the eye. You had "Yes, please" and "No, thank you" down cold. And you knew to send thank you notes for any gift or kind gesture from others. Because you'd learned so much about boundaries, rules, manners, and expectations, we didn't need much reinforcement anymore.

I've written in this book about my feelings toward the private school you attended your first two years of middle school. When you started your first year, we had the opportunity to teach you about the areas in which our rules for life differed from those set down by the school. You knew that homework was your responsibility, showing respect for your teachers was imperative. You also knew that you needed to be mindful of the rules your school set in place, even if you didn't agree with them. I think there's a difference between being mindful and standing up for what you believe. I mean this school was proud of teaching kids to become critical thinkers. They encouraged questioning. Yet they didn't seem so hot on the idea of the kids questioning them, even when done with respect.

They weren't so hot on the adults questioning them either. Each year, you were supposed to have three weekends (holiday weekends) without homework. One year, one of your teachers decided to assign homework anyway. It may not seem like a big deal to some, but we had a busy holiday schedule, so we went to speak to the principal. Well, let's just say that it didn't go well. She felt that we needed to be flexible. And we felt it was important to stick to the promises they'd made to the kids. She didn't cave, and we had to cancel many of our holiday plans. One more place where our family values and the school's values were completely different.

I've said that we were all for you learning a lot and having the discipline, fortitude, and ability for doing your homework, BUT—and this is a REALLY BIG BUT—we thought there was more to life than just school. Work-life balance is something that's hard to achieve, but it seems mighty important to work toward. My boss says it doesn't exist, but I would counter that it does. It's just a very delicate balance. So, as I'm sure you remember, we sat down as a family and worked out solutions for finding you a better fit for eighth grade. It was during these conversations that we figured out that you liked public school much better than private because of its diversity, convenience, and access to friends who lived close by. You then decided that after middle school, you'd go to a public high school.

At this age, we were clear we didn't want you to grow up too fast. We were sticklers about wearing age-appropriate clothing, watching age-appropriate movies, and listening to age-appropriate music. We also ruled out makeup. I knew that I wanted to preserve your childhood for as long as possible. We knew you would have plenty of time to be an adult. I told you that if one of your friends ever asked you to do something that made you uncomfortable, you could use us as an excuse, saying, "My parents won't let me," so that you could let us be the mean ones. I have no idea how many times blaming us helped, but I imagine it was a relief to know that we had your back.

This seems as good a time as any to work in one of my favorite rules, one I've taught you since you were little: Do unto others as you would have them do unto you. Need I say more?!

Ages fourteen through eighteen

With high school came more freedom, as long as you observed the rules. By this time, you understood our expectations, and we trusted you and your choices, so high school was a breeze as far as our relationship was concerned. It's never too late to work on boundaries, rules, and manners, *but* the later you start, the steeper the learning curve. Some of the rules at this stage were that schoolwork came before extra-curricular activities. However, if you were on a team, you signed up to commit to that team, and you followed through. You had learned that one a long time ago. Remember when you were five or six and wanted to quit the T-ball team, and we said, "Sorry kiddo. You need to finish what you started?" We'd laid the foundation, so during high school, you were simply building on what was already in place.

You would get homework out of the way so you could enjoy extracurricular activities. Between school, sports, and time with friends and family you learned the importance of budgeting time. You *really* were a breeze in high school. I know you've heard this before, but I think one of the reasons we didn't have that many fallouts in high school is because you ate organic most of your life so the extra hormones that the food industry adds to foods did not have you experiencing the mood swings that sometimes affected other kids. Just my theory.

As you remember, we set curfews, and I did my best to get to know your friends and have an open door policy. You knew to respect yourself and others, to take responsibility for yourself. You felt a responsibility to the community. You knew there'd be natural consequences when and if you ignored the boundaries. We did our best to have you understand that feeling "invincible ignorance" is not a good thing. You know what I'm talking about. That feeling teens get that they're invincible, where they seem to be totally ignorant of the fact that they aren't. They often take ridiculous risks as a result.

We did face a new challenge in high school—parties where alcohol was served. I'm sure drugs were part of the scene, too. Some of our parent peers would be the ones hosting the drinking parties. As you know, we didn't host any—we didn't want to be accomplices to underage drinking. If we did, we felt we were lowering a moral and ethical bar by allowing illegal activities and, in turn, teaching you that it would be okay to break the law. Also the research shows that your brain is not fully formed until you're twenty-one, and alcohol can do it damage.

Remember how our family friend Groucho told you that taking drugs had changed his chemistry and added to his paranoia? He said he really wanted you to consider the option of not doing any recreational drugs. And, you know my story of never having tried any of them. I wasn't a saint. I just wasn't interested. Besides, I already drank too much in high school. Thank goodness booze was not your escape mechanism. You father and I were always honest about our teen years and the mistakes we made. We shared our mistakes with the hope that you would choose not to repeat them.

You did like to attend parties, though, so we had discussions about what would happen if the police busted the party for underage drinking or drugs. Thankfully, that never occurred. You also knew that if you ever did drink, you should phone home for a safe ride. I remember a night when you went to a party, and you and another sober friend saw how there was absolutely no way your friends who had been drinking could drive a car. So you took their keys and drove quite a few of them home. You saw how impaired your friends were. You realized how invincible they felt, with no idea they were so messed up. I think that night really drove (sorry) the point home to you—don't drink and drive.

One more important discussion we had with you during this time was about how to not move your ethical markers. In high school, the pressure can become intense, so markers get moved. But if you do it once, they will continue to get moved and it will be increasingly harder to find your ethics in the future.

Here's an example that you'll get a kick out of. When I started this book I found an incredible quote that I wanted to use in the beginning of the book. This author is also a father, and I thought the words I wanted to quote were loving, inspired, and profound. You, dad, and I had attended one of the author's lectures some time ago. I thought he was great, but you and dad felt he was a bit sketchy. I told you I was quoting him in the book, and you were dead against it.

After I'd finished my first draft, sent it to friends, and was incorporating their feedback, I found out this man was indicted for a felony. I had to take the quote out of the book. I was sad for all who would never hear this quote. I was sad for the example he was modeling for his children. And, above all, I was sad that at some point in his life he had started moving his ethical markers. All that he could have shared was marred by some very bad choices.

I have to say, though, I found it amusing that when I was telling you this story, you weren't surprised and almost felt vindicated that your intuition was right. Always trust your intuition. You said that you didn't trust this man and weren't surprised by his actions. You know me, I always expect the best from everyone and I hold them all to a high but reachable standard, and my trust of everyone starts at that high point.

I love the way you stick to your principles and stand up for what you believe in. The other day, I was thinking about the time you left school to attend a rally you were passionate about. The rally was a protest against the war in Iraq. Many students attended. I sent a note to the school excusing your absence but the principal called back saying he would not excuse your absence. I respected what you were doing. I told him I would call the ACLU, and he finally backed off.

When you were fifteen, your dad made an exchange with one of his clients who needed some body work done on his car in exchange for a car he wanted to get rid of, he thought your dad might want the car. It was a bright orange 1974 BMW 2002. Your dad thought it would be a great car for you. At first I was opposed to the idea of providing you with a car but, after much discussion, I saw your dad's point of view. He thought that you needed a stick shift, so that you'd be more present when driving. I liked the bright orange color, because your car would stand out and if you were doing something outside the rules, the police would notice. I remember asking friends and neighbors to keep their eyes out for you. If they saw anyone in your car during the six-month probation period, when you could only drive by yourself or with another adult, to let me know. One day, a dear friend called to tell me she'd just seen your car, and there were two people it in. Thank goodness for her call. And, thank goodness it was me in the passenger seat! I know another woman who wrote up a contract about following the driving rules during the probation period. Both she and her daughter signed it. I loved that idea! I'm all about clarity.

During your junior year, when it came time to decide which colleges you wanted to apply to, your dad and I both agreed we weren't going to haul you all over the country to visit each college that interested you. The idea was totally foreign to us. We felt you needed to own your college search, hopefully online if the school was out of state. When the college recruiter came to your high school, you decided The Global College of Long Island was for you. You liked the idea of experiential learning while traveling to mostly third world countries. When you decided there was only one college for you, we had a conversation about what would happen if you didn't get in. You said, "I'll take a gap year and reapply next year." If you needed to try a third time, you'd do that too. Clearly, you'd learned that it's not how many times you fall down, it's how many times you get back up.

Also, in our view, it was not our responsibility to pay for your entire college education. As you've heard us say throughout your life, we felt you needed to have skin in the game—whether it was by working, searching and applying for loans and grants, work study, whatever you could do to help. Having skin in the game will make your life richer and prepare you for the responsibility of the "real world." Good luck defining the "real world."

Nurturing Body and Soul

Yuck!

You were NEVER allowed to use that word to describe food when you were little. As your vocabulary grew, you knew it was unacceptable to make any derogatory remarks about the meals prepared for you.

My childhood relationship with good, healthful food started when I was very young. Grandma Carol used to make homemade bread once a week. She was a fabulous cook, so we grew up with an array of healthful food. Once a year, if we were doing well in school and our attendance was good, she'd reward us by taking us out to lunch at the place of our choosing. I loved a good restaurant, even back then.

When I was in the seventh and eighth grade, we moved to Brussels, where my love for food developed even further. Europeans know how to dine—a meal is an event. Food is something that feeds your body and soul. And the feeding of one's soul is of equal importance to feeding one's body. I suggest teaching your child to do both.

When I started this book, I thought this chapter would be one of the easiest. As I began to write it, I found that offering you tips and guidance for feeding your child's body was a breeze, but describing where a child's soul could veer from a safe path was not so easy. For me, a soul is the part of you other than flesh, bones, or your brain. A soul can shatter in the blink of an eye for so many reasons, including abuse, neglect, non-acceptance, or other life-altering events. The good news is that when a soul is nurtured and cherished, it can grow in unbelievable ways. And, it can be healed.

Temple Grandin, a successful doctor and author who was diagnosed with autism, is a perfect example of a person whose soul was fully and beautifully nurtured, and as a result, she made invaluable contributions, helping to make our world a far, far better place. Because of Temple's understanding of the world she lived in, and because of her affinity for animals and her passion for animal rights, she was able to design an entirely new slaughtering system—one that included curved corrals, or pathways, intended to reduce stress in the animals being led to slaughter. We would never have had her contributions and her special insights if not for her mother's amazing nurturing, her awareness of how her daughter was going to function in a world so "foreign" to her.

We wanted to start teaching you about your soul very, very early. So while I struggled to make sure that even as a child you understood the gravity of your soul's journey, I did something I often do, I talked to others. I studied life and the humans around me, and reflected on all that I saw and heard. One person told me that to protect the soul and help it expand and flourish, the soul needs only to be loved with pure, nonjudgmental love. Another person said that a soul is like a hollyhock flower. It just needs good dirt, water, sunlight, air, and the right kind of care to grow up feeling loved and nurtured, to flourish and fully bloom.

Then I heard a lovely story about a young woman who was dying (way too young) and how full of love she and her family were during the process of watching her slip away. Her friend described her in such wonderful detail—how everyone loved and cherished her, how she was honest and open and wore her heart on her sleeve, how she embraced and fully engaged with life and the people she encountered. She shared her love and her soul. If we do nothing else in this life but honestly and openly share our soul with others, I believe the world will be a better place, a beautiful place.

I have another story, one that's more recent. While I was in downtown Seattle, I met a homeless woman. After I parked my car, this woman walked toward me to say hello. She looked about 70 years old. She nodded hello and flashed a broad smile that showed her two teeth. I went to do my errand. When I returned, she was sitting against a building on the sidewalk next to my car. She mumbled something that I couldn't understand, so I walked over to her to hear her better.

I asked her to repeat her request, and she asked if I had any change. I opened my wallet and said that I didn't, but I had a dollar bill. "Would that work?" Once again, she flashed her nearly toothless grin. Sure, she was happy about the dollar and I loved her grin, but I'll never forget what happened after I gave her the money and she smiled again. I try to keep Compendium window message cards in my glove box, so that when I meet others, I have a way to brighten their day. These cards are about 2¼" square, small enough to carry with you in your wallet. They come in many different varieties. The sayings on the ones I had that day were Spirit, Love, Dream, and Hope. The inside contains a corresponding message.

So I opened the glove box and grabbed one of each, and then started to explain how these little treasures worked. We chose to open Hope first. I showed her how to open the die-cut window to reveal the message inside. The message to her was such a gift to us both. It said, "You are not a victim. You are a person with a lot of experience." Oh my, how she smiled and laughed and went on about how much experience she had. As I drove away, I saw her opening the next message. Our encounter was a blessing for us both. I received the pleasure of her smile, laughter, and beautiful eyes. I also got the chance to meet a woman who was not a victim, despite her experiences, many of which I'm sure were tough. And, she received information that seemed clearly to hit home.

I'll continue to spread these little notes of encouragement far and wide. You know, until I was writing this story, I'd forgotten how, when you were little, I would put little tiny cards with words of encouragement in your lunchbox, sports-bag, backpack, and suitcase. I guess seeing how that worked with you helped me to carry on the tradition with random strangers. Interesting how something so small and seemingly separate becomes clearly connected.

Something that I know you learned from me was to speak respectfully with others no matter who they are. Or, put another way, you could say, "I've never met a stranger." I know that while you were an undergrad attending school in South Africa, you wrote about the way in which South Africans address each other with such ease, even when they don't know one another. Tonight, as your dad and I sat on a park bench overlooking Puget Sound, I was thinking about your words and how maybe I'd just been born on the wrong continent because of my overtly friendly nature. I told your dad what I was thinking, and his very kind response was filled with such strength and beauty. He turned my thoughts sideways. Here's what he said. "Maybe you were born in the right place so you could teach us how to speak to one another as non-strangers and, moreover, you needed to be here for us to meet, for Carly to be born." Boy, did I marry well.

As far as your soul and its growth were concerned, I figured this job would be done by nurturing, protecting (when possible—it wasn't always possible, as you know), modeling, and loving who you were, as you were. We also tried helping you to grow your strengths whenever we could.

I thought that the bond and acceptance between you and your dad would give your soul the wings it would need to soar. Please don't misunderstand me, Carly, my relationship with you was equally important. I just think that a strong, accepting, and respectful relationship between a father and daughter helps young women become their best most confident selves. This is not to say that every girl needs a father, but in my opinion, a strong male mentor is such a gift to a young woman's self-confidence.

Even before you were conceived, your dad and I knew that nurturing your body and soul would be a primary concern for us. As our very dear friend Barbara says, "Our only job in life is to grow our soul." I will add, the best way to do this is to make sure that your body has the right fuel so that you can concentrate on growing your soul.

I've been on the organic food train for a long time. Because of the toxins involved in your dad's work, I've tried to keep the toxins in our home to a minimum. Your dad and I joined PCC food co-op when we first moved in together, and two years after you were born we joined our beloved community supported agriculture (CSA). The farm-fresh food that Helsing Junction Farms delivers to us weekly has been such a blessing each year, spring through fall. As I've said before, I know in my heart of hearts that the reason for your limited mood swings in adolescence was due to your being fed organic, sustainable, mostly local food. It was free of any added hormones, thank goodness.

Food took a large chunk out of our budget. We were lucky to have the ability to make this a priority, but we did have to sacrifice in other areas to make this choice. As you know, I often think long and hard about my choices and their consequences. I'll give you my big picture first, the little picture second.

The big picture is that the Earth is sacred and should be treated with respect and not poisoned. The little picture is that we should not support others who poison the earth and poison every living thing on this planet. Many might think that human beings are the big picture, but I would heartily disagree. Many species have become extinct . . . and the earth is still here. Unfortunately, we humans have taken a toll on our planet. But I have hopes that your generation will put Earth and peoples' health before corporate and Wall Street profits. As you may remember I have been forever talking with you about voting with one's wallet.

Another influence on my ideals about nurturing your body and soul was my experience with the Christian Science tradition. I'm not sure if I have the beliefs exactly right, but the essence of what I remember is that your body and soul are temples and should be treated as such. Because I believe that our souls are here to learn lessons and move forward to new ones, I believe that our souls need to be nurtured to be ready for those lessons.

We needed to nurture you and teach you how to nurture yourself. If you learned how to nurture yourself, you would in turn know that you were worthy of kindness, friendship, deep relationships, love, and all that life has to offer. I think your worth and value are connected to how you relate to your soul. When you look at yourself now, Carly, I know you know that you are worthy. I know you know you can accomplish anything you have a passion for. That said, I know above all else that you know you are not your accomplishments. You are your heart and soul. It's really important to know who you are. From my perspective your soul is, among other things, strong, compassionate, gentle, tender, old, and wise.

It's important to work with our children so they can make the connections between feeding their body and nurturing their soul. Here are a few questions that might help your child. "If I don't treat my body well how will it treat me?" "If my body isn't sustained, how will it operate?" "If my body isn't well cared for, what's the message to my soul about my respect for myself?" "If I don't nourish my soul will I have anything to give to myself or others?"

I know that nurturing your child's body and soul will work well for you and your family. As for the body, our love of food has been handed down for generations. Regarding the soul, my modeling of how I nourish my soul has been front and center for some time. Your gift for treating your body and soul well has taught your dad and me a thing or two. For instance, I love the deodorant that you make for me with those three simple ingredients (baking soda, corn flour, and coconut oil). You've taken the lack of consumption to levels that I hadn't even considered.

A soul is a very tender part of our children, and I think sometimes parents think that giving trophies and over-praising their children's intelligence, gifts, or athletic abilities nourishes their souls. But, I *do not* believe this is true. I know (and have seen) that children understand the difference between souls that are nourished and expanding and those that are not, and nourishment usually doesn't relate to material goods or excessive praise. It's vital that we do everything possible as a community to make sure children's souls are cherished, nurtured, and grown. As I've said, a soul can be shattered in an instant. The repairing of a soul is difficult at best, and sometimes seemingly impossible. I believe that the stronger the soul, the greater the possibility for healing any wounds that may occur. So, please, do everything in your power to nurture your child's soul.

Above all else, remember to teach your child that trying to fill the emptiness of one's soul is never accomplished by gaining approval from others, winning competitions, purchasing gadgets/homes/cars, accumulating wealth, or exercising power over others.

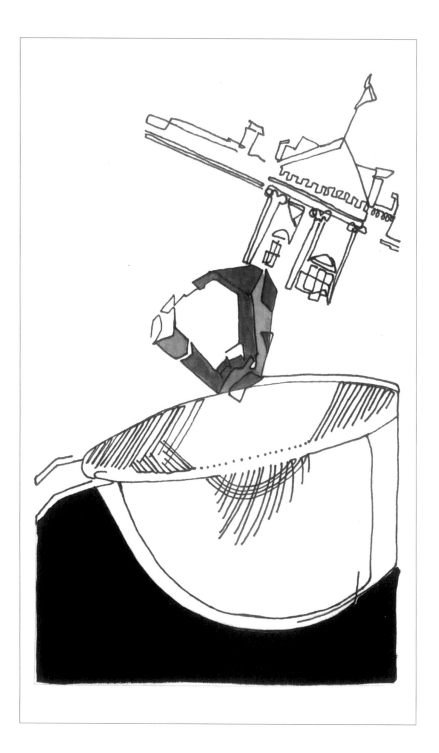

Birth through age two

Breast milk... sounds so simple. But for us (and others) it wasn't. You weren't good at latching on, and my body didn't make it easy. When we left the hospital, you and I had no idea how to make things better, and they continued to get worse. When I'd try to nurse, the pain was overwhelming, and I was just about to throw in the towel. I didn't want to give up, because I knew how important breast milk was, and I hated the idea of formula. But I knew I couldn't take the pain. I felt so alone and inept.

Thankfully for us, your aunt Blythe was in town. She was a leader in La Leche League, so she was a pro at problem-solving for breastfeeding. Your cousin Kitty was with her. Since Kitty is just six months older than you are, swapping babies was easy (an idea that Blythe came up with but La Leche League would never suggest). We exchanged babies to breastfeed, so that I got the hang of how it felt when it was done "correctly," and you got the idea of how to latch on. With just a few tips, you and I were good to go, and breastfeeding went great from then on.

This may sound really weird, kiddo, but the swapping made it possible for me to breastfeed you. As I've said before our village was large, present, and accounted for. Just recently one of my co-worker's wives was having the same problem that I had, and boy did it feel good to encourage her by sharing our story. I think it helped her to realize she wasn't alone and to learn about La Leche League, a place where she could go for help.

I was able to give you breast milk for as long as possible. It was tricky because I worked. I had a lot of meetings, and I went on business trips. Back then breast pumps were expensive and way too large to be portable (boy, have things changed), so we rented one and kept it at home. I planned my business appointments around pumping time. Before I traveled, I pumped milk for you to drink while I was gone. This was a bit of a hassle, but being a parent means learning to adjust your expectations about what your life should or could look like.

I was blessed with a job that was flexible enough to allow for pumping, and we were committed to the best nutrition possible for you, which we believed was my milk. Later, you learned to love the bottle, because you had an easier time getting your milk. Pumping my milk was a great way for you to drink from the bottle without having to drink formula. As you grew, we followed your doctor's thoughts about when to add cereal and solid foods. Of course those foods were all organic. There were very few foods you wouldn't eat, thank goodness. You've always liked good food.

As for nurturing your soul during this time—you were loved, cherished, and adored. You had two fabulous nannies between birth and age two. Maffe was with us for your first year and Ivona was with us during your second. Maffe loved you like a little sister, and she fed your soul with her gentle kindness. Ivona agreed that fresh food was a top priority, with fresh air coming in a close second. So, every day she made fresh soup, piroshkies, or some other very healthful meal for you. We always knew we could count on Ivona to feed your body and soul with love, attention, great food, and a healthy dose of outside exercise and walks.

While we're on the subject of nannies, I've always believed they taught me how to be the best mom possible for you. They also gave me time to hone my mothering skills. I know that you would not have been as nourished today without the help of these amazing women. I believe I was a good mom to you at this stage, and I know these women helped me become a better one. Again, this is my experience. I know that not everyone can afford nannies. My point is that I think it's extremely important for the parents and the child to seek out others for both information and socialization, for them to interact with others outside the home.

Ages three through five

Nanny sharing was a great help to our family. This worked within our budget. As a single child, being around other children and in their homes, helped you to expand your perspective of the world. When and if you decide that nanny sharing is for your family, here are a few things you might want to consider. What are your thoughts about how the children are entertained? What are your priorities?

For example, does your family have a reading time every day? Are there traditions that are shared by both families? How many children do you think a nanny can be present with and what kind of rules, manners, and discipline do you think are important? For us, food and exercise/outdoor time also played a large part in the equation. Some caretakers were better matches than others. Some nannies lasted a day, some a week or two, but the best ones lasted a year or more. Finding that fit wasn't always easy for the nanny or the families involved. But finding the right fit was always worth the effort and energy.

When you were about three years old, we found your third and final nanny. Shelli was terrific with love, discipline, food, nutrition, exercise, outside time, and creativity. Shelli really connected with you and got who you were and might become. She was a master at nannying, as was her mother. These women had a gift that we were lucky to have shared with us. We received the gift of Shelli's mother's knowledge through Shelli.

While Shelli was with us, you learned so many things about caring for your body. She taught you from a very young age about healthful snacks, brushing your teeth well, and (when you were about to enter kindergarten, right before we no longer needed her to work full time) she taught you how to make your own breakfast.

I remember asking her if she thought it was necessary for a kindergartener to make her own breakfast. She was clear as a bell when she told me you were perfectly capable, and if you made your own breakfast, we'd have more quality time together before school. Boy was she right. You learned how to take care of yourself first thing in the morning. It was wonderful to see what you were capable of when allowed to stretch and grow into independence. And, our time before school was much better. You got yourself ready while I got myself ready, and then our walk to school was more peaceful.

Meals were also easier. You made your own breakfast. Since your dad made your lunches, two meals were taken care of, leaving dinner to me. What a great community effort it was—making meals. Being a parent requires tremendous organizational skills. So being responsible for one meal only was such a gift.

Shelli focused on nourishing your soul in everything you did, especially by creating art projects with you and exploring nature, both of which you were passionate about. You were extremely creative, and she fostered that aspect of who you were. As you created or explored the world she never hurried you, she never dictated. She started with a blank canvas, so that your art and clarity about your art became your own, as did your view of nature. I saw how art and nature fed your soul at that age. Encouraging all types of learning can develop the mind and soul.

Nature also fed our bodies and our souls. Walks and bike rides, skiing, time spent on the beaches and in the mountains—we were so lucky to live in a place with so many opportunities for nourishment. I know that wherever you live, you'll find the places that feed your body and soul, and those of your family as well.

So here I go, back on the healthful food soapbox. Once again, I'll say how strongly I feel about good nutrition. I firmly believe that fueling the body helps build the mind and nurtures the body so there's room to focus on and expand your soul. When you were able to eat what we did, we started to expand the types of food you ate. You always had to try something first before deciding you didn't like it. You tried everything that was made available and, with the exception of asparagus, I can't think of anything you didn't like.

We were lucky, because you weren't a fussy eater. Though if you had been, we just would have had to try new tactics. I'm not sure what those would have been. I probably would have found out by following my usual routine—asking and listening to those around me. Dinner was a balance of veggies, proteins, and fruits. I didn't want you filling up on bread, so we ate bread after we finished the more nutritious part of the meal.

Since I wasn't raised on pop and chips, you weren't either (unless I was traveling and dad was in charge ☺). I always made fruit and veggies available for snacking. We rarely, if ever, had dessert.

I have a friend, who is also a client, who shared a great story with me about his kids. Before his kids ate a sugary snack (often when they were on outings), he and his wife used to ask them to picture and imagine how it would feel to eat, chew, and swallow the treat. Those who thought it would be fine were told to go for it, but those who thought any part of the process might make them feel yucky or sick to their tummy were encouraged not to eat the snack. At the point we talked, he said his kids were old enough to do this exercise without prompting, and they made great choices. What a great parenting tip!

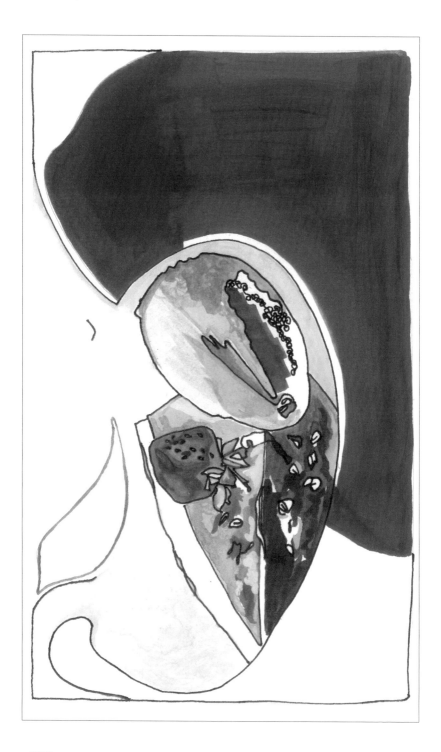

I know you'll remember the time that one of your friends came to dinner and cried most of the way through the meal because he was used to eating bread and pasta with butter for dinner. That night, we weren't having either of those items. Try as I might, this child did not understand the concept of his health being directly connected to what he ate. To this day, I think about him and hope he looked back on that dinner and something clicked. I hope he got the connection between healthful foods and a healthy body. If he hasn't made the connection yet, I hope he will.

I always enjoyed having your friends to dinner. Eating together and sharing our love as a family, nourished our souls, and we were always happy to share our love and nutrition with others. By sharing meals, we nourished our own souls and the souls of our company—friends, loved ones, and sometimes people we didn't even know.

Ages six through ten

School, nutrition, sleep, and the nurturing of your kid's soul will require a great deal of juggling and organization to find the right balance. To maintain this balance, your family will need to be especially mindful, noting when one element might be out of whack. Your dad and I knew that if you were hungry or tired, life didn't go well for you (or those around you!). So you and I worked out what you liked and could fix yourself for breakfast, and you and dad worked out the details of what you two thought would work for lunches.

Speaking of lunches, I knew that you left the house each day with a good, healthful lunch. I also knew that you and your friends sometimes traded food. I think you liked trading, and maybe you were trading for items that I wouldn't have served you, but I knew I couldn't control everything you put in your mouth, and I didn't want to. I also trusted for the most part you'd make good choices, and I'm sure that exchanging food taught you some negotiation skills. Good for all of you.

When it came to snacks after school and after dinner, there was always fruit in the fruit bowl for you to eat. You also knew and were reminded not to snack too close to dinner time. You and dad were well aware that cooking dinner for me was not only a meditation of sorts but also a passion that I wanted to share with one and all and I wanted you two to be hungry and ready to enjoy. If you filled up on snacks wrecking the dinner I'd so lovingly prepared, it wouldn't be pretty.

At this stage, if you'd been a picky eater, we might have tried to get you to enjoy new foods by letting you make healthful dinners for yourself occasionally, but they would have had to have been healthful. I think that picky eaters might be made that way rather than born that way. So, Carly, if your child is a picky eater, you might want to involve him or her in grocery shopping, menu planning, and cooking meals. Try taking some cooking classes together. I think once you engage kids in the process, they might learn to appreciate healthful food more and even realize how much better they feel when they eat well. Who knows? And if this doesn't work, send your child to grandma's (my) house, and I'll ever so happily help connect these dots.

Sleep is critical to health. To help you maintain your balance, you had a set bedtime, one that was rarely moved. It would have been really nice to move our boundaries to take advantage of more social and extra-curricular opportunities. If we'd been more flexible in this area we could have all had more fun! Who doesn't like to take advantage of the social, educational, and creative opportunities that come their way?

I think sticking to a specific bedtime for their kids can be hard for many parents, but we didn't feel giving you a flexible bedtime was the right thing to do. And, it wasn't right for you. You needed sleep, and I believe the research in this area backs me up. We stood by a firm bedtime and, in the end, that decision not only made our lives work better and helped our balancing act, but it also helped our family to prioritize items on our social calendar. For example, if there was a special movie that we all wanted to see and it lasted past your bed time, we'd wait until the weekend to see it as a matinée.

Learning to prioritize was a great thing for you to start learning at this age. You also learned to weigh the consequences of committing to an activity. For example, if one friend would ask you to do something fun and then a better "more fun" opportunity would arise, you were never allowed to jump ship.

This age was filled with opportunities to build upon and learn more about our family's morals, values, and expectations. We were clear that we wanted you to get to be a little kid as long as possible, so you had very little exposure to "older kids' stuff." I'd say one of our biggest challenges was age-appropriate clothing. We were sticklers about your wearing clothing suitable to your age, but it was tough to find those clothes.

You were really tall for your age. During these years you shot up so fast that you had a hard time sometimes finding your center of gravity, and the growing pains weren't fun either. Finding age-appropriate clothing was super frustrating. To accommodate your height, we had to shop for clothing for kids much older than you and that clothing was not at all suitable for someone your age. You were always clear that you had your own style, and we were good with that. We just didn't feel it was okay to objectify you. You also had to deal with peer pressure. When you were in third and fourth grade, many of your friends wore clothing that we weren't about to let you wear. I'm not sure if you ever resented this, but I'm super comfortable with the choices and rules we made about this for you.

One last thing about your body at this age. When you were in upper elementary school, you started to get a bit rounder. I remember your grandma Carol being troubled by your weight gain. I had to strongly remind her on many occasions that your body was right on track. Your body was gaining weight to get ready for puberty. I've talked with a number of women who were teased and taunted by fathers, mothers, siblings, and friends while experiencing slight weight gain during their pre-pubescent years. None of these women felt the teasing and taunting helped in any way. Many even said they can still feel the pain many years later. I'm sure you'll be mindful to help your child love his or her body as it changes throughout childhood.

Your soul continued to be nurtured by creating pieces of art, playing sports, and participating in outdoor adventures. You had some terrific mentors for all of these activities. Mentoring brings up a great and important subject. Since nannies were no longer necessary, mentors, babysitters, and close family friends were super important for nurturing your soul. The other day, I ran into one of your dear friends and her mom, who thanked me for mentoring her daughter. She said she wondered why, when her daughter was young, she and I could say the exact same thing and her daughter would listen to me instead of her. Kids are like that. They'll often listen to someone else's advice but can't hear or won't listen to the same advice from their parents. But they need to talk, so mentors and friends are really important. Again, it takes a village. Find people who will do this for your child.

Ages eleven through thirteen

You still needed nutrition and sleep to be at your best. Your middle school had amazing school lunches, one of the perks of private school. But our budget was an issue for us, so as I remember, you still packed your lunch most of the time. The sleep part was tough due to ALL the HOMEWORK! Can you say balance?

Carly, when and if you ever send your kids to private school, please, please, please explore the options. Study each school very carefully. With the growth of charter schools, you'll certainly have more choices. I'm not necessarily endorsing charter schools, I'm just saying I think you'll have more educational options for your child. Not too long ago, you spoke about opening a school with a college friend. Maybe you will. And, who knows? Maybe that's where your child will go?!

I think because your soul was cherished and fiercely protected up to this point, you started to learn how to protect it yourself. I think one of a parent's many important jobs is to protect and nurture their kids' souls, to show kids how to cherish their own souls, to watch them to see if they've "got it," and then guide them when needed. By this age you, knew that you needed sports to help you unwind, art and music to find your center, and outdoor time with us to connect with the earth.

Ages fourteen through eighteen

By now, you were involved in all the high school sports available to you. Unlike select soccer, which was not a school sport and would have eaten all our time, participating in high school sports did not take up our lives or eat up our dinner time (pun intended). You knew that to play your best, to keep up, you needed to be in tip-top shape, so you treated food and your body with respect. You brought after-school snacks to eat before your games or practice. You worked on drinking enough water, though you needed reminders! I think you had an athlete's body, so your body image was good, or as good as it could be in high school for a girl in the United States. I'll refrain from lecturing about media-generated body expectations. I don't think you want to hear that again, do you?

By high school, you were really taking charge of your own health and eager to help others. You worked on nutrition with the kids you babysat. I always loved hearing about how you got kids to eat food that was really good for them but that they didn't want to eat. When I saw how you took care of your body as an athlete and how you made sure the kids you took care of ate well, I realized that you clearly needed no more help in this area. You were good to go.

You also joined in the cooking at home. When you come home from school to visit, I love the fellowship but I also love eating the wonderful food that you prepare. When you started cooking for us when you were in college, I could see how much you loved it. You've only gotten better. You've become an amazing cook. I so appreciate and love the food you prepare, so does your dad.

I've talked about limiting screen time. You didn't own a video game until you were eighteen and your uncle gave you that really old one. To us, social networking (Myspace and Facebook) fell into the screen time category. When you were in high school, we felt that relating and communicating person-to-person fed a part of your soul that couldn't be touched by virtual interaction. I also know limiting virtual relationships helped you develop strong interpersonal skills. So, remember to be mindful in these areas.

I remember when you were in your first years of college, and you shut down your Facebook account because you found it to be "unreal." Carly, hold that memory tight when thinking about how you want to structure your own child's involvement with electronic interaction. With the speed that technology is morphing and advancing, I think your choices will be completely different from those we faced. You probably won't be able to restrict screen time but the basic principles I've talked about will still hold true.

I've never believed in hiding my childhood mistakes from you. I told the good, the bad, and the ugly when it was age-appropriate for you. My high school years were rough. My soul wasn't protected, and I looked for approval in all the wrong places. While I didn't objectify myself with what I wore, I was promiscuous. Not one of my better choices.

Carly, I never want you to experience it firsthand, yet I want you to understand how horrible it feels to make choices that cause you to lose respect for yourself. I'm talking about wearing clothes that objectify you and acting a certain way that doesn't reflect who you really are—especially when you send the wrong message to boys or men just to get their attention, as if you don't believe who you are is enough.

When you were in high school, the good news was, I was able to talk with you, your friends, and other neighborhood girls about what I'd learned from my own experiences. Our home was a safe place to come and chat about the problems and realities of growing up into womanhood. Thankfully, none of these young girls (that I know of) ever had to make the tough decision that one my high school friends and many women I knew had to make—to have or not have an abortion. I'm so glad that the subject of birth control is now so out in the open.

Furthermore, because of my AIDS volunteer work prior to your birth, I was clear with one and all that having sex meant wearing condoms. I did not encourage or condone pre-marital/high school sex, but I wasn't living in a box either. I know that the definition of sexual acts changes. Sexual practices change. Terminology changes, too. When my neighbor (who is now in her fifties) was in sixth grade, she cried to her mom that she was the only one in her class who'd never made out with a boy. Her mom freaked. In her mom's day "making out" had meant having full on sex. My neighbor had been talking about kissing.

Anyway, definitions, practices, and standards will change as you grow up, so try to stay in touch. I knew you and your friends needed a safe place to talk. Oddly, thankfully, and luckily, the two gals that you hung out with the most didn't date in high school. I was glad that you all attended the dances, football games, and parties, but I was even more pleased that none of you needed a guy's approval or endorsement to affirm your self-worth.

While I was mentoring some of those great girls, I remember teaching them a couple key points. One point was: *I can't care more about your life than you do.* So, if they started to hang out at our house and needed help with something, I was all in as long as they made the commitment to be all in too. We would enter into a no bullshit agreement. I taught you girls one of my mantras: *You can either be pitiful or powerful, but you can't be both.* When one of these girls tried on the role of being a victim, I reminded her that being a strong woman was much more interesting and empowering.

I spoke with most of these girls, because their parents asked me to. They came over and we chatted. You were peripherally involved in watching my mentoring, so you got to see what it looked like when someone else protected their soul. I'm thankful for all the time we got to spend together. I've often said that, if possible, it's really important to be home after school during your kid's high school years.

I had another client/friend tell me that when she was in school, her father yelled at her for getting F's instead of helping her to achieve A's. I know that parents can (and I did at times) equate their kids value/worth with their grades. But, by all means, do your level best not to. When your kids do their best at their school work, they should know that their best is exactly that. Their best.

None of us are good at everything. So what if math is tough and English is easy? When kids give their all, it's really important for parents to let them know they have their backs. As long as they tried their best, they're golden. It's also important to encourage them to take part in activities they love, that nourish them, and at which they can succeed. By standing behind their kids when they try their best, parents can help their children develop beautiful, strong souls.

I know this was true for you.

Exploring the World

YES!

I love the word "yes." I say it often and with enthusiasm. There are people to meet, places to go, foods to taste, countries to explore, cultures to understand, and traditions to learn. I think I've always had a hunger to learn by experiencing life. For as long as I can remember, I was curious about EVERYTHING! If you ask grandma, she might describe me as an annoyingly curious "why" child. To this day, when I'm in a conversation, I'm always asking questions—"Why this?" and "How that?"

I'm interested in knowing people's stories. I want to know why they believe and act the way they do, and why human nature can be so diverse. As you've witnessed, even when I'm not asking questions, people tend to tell me their stories. So when it came to raising you, you were exposed to and immersed in an array of diverse people, cultures, traditions, places, and types of food.

Your dad and I have had a cast of characters in our lives. I met one of our most authentic friends, Groucho, when he was homeless and I was opening a business in his at-that-time neighborhood. We have friends who have never traveled at all, who've never strayed from Washington State. And, we have dear friends who've traveled the world most of their lives. Take Mitch, who not only travels for business

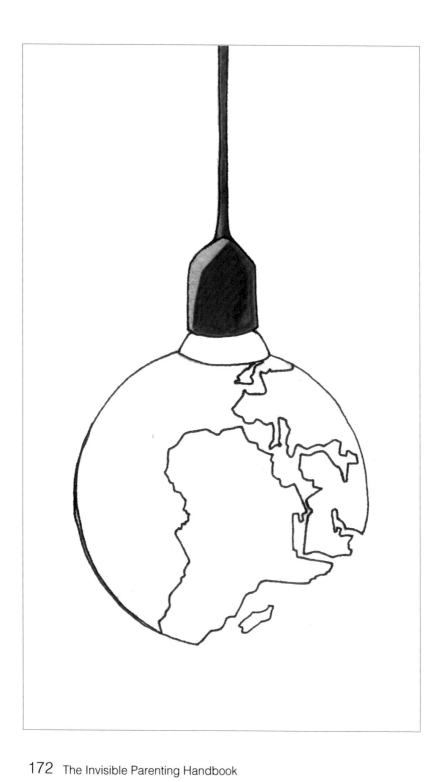

but also for pleasure. He's a travel junkie. Mitch always makes me think of a great quote by Mark Twain, "Travel is fatal to prejudice, bigotry, and narrow-mindedness."

I absolutely understand that travel can be a luxury many can't afford, especially when the trips are far from home. We had to think long and hard about the trips you took. (We're still paying off one of them.) But the world is a much smaller place than it was when Mark Twain expressed his feelings about the importance of travel. Communities are far more diverse.

There are so many opportunities to help your child discover the world. In addition to books and watching films, you can drive to other neighborhoods, join community centers, and give time to various nonprofits. You can often learn an enormous amount from families on your block or in your apartment building. And if your child wants to travel farther, he or she might volunteer for an organization that covers travel expenses.

Carly, when you were really young, we traveled as much as we could afford and as often as was reasonable for your age. We didn't have the funds to travel abroad or to faraway places. So we traveled within the states, visiting friends, family members, and even some of my bosses. Sometimes these bosses, who'd become friends, invited us to stay with them. You and your dad would also accompany me on some of my business trips. We went to fun locations like California, New York, Kansas, Arkansas, Connecticut, Alabama, and Vancouver, Canada. I could be pretty clever at gathering free miles and stretching our travel dollars, and those who we visited were always generous and offered lodging in their homes, condos, and apartments.

I remember when I told people that we went on a vacation to Kansas or Arkansas, they'd involuntarily laugh or smirk, BUT believe you me, those trips were AWESOME! They were filled with adventure. On those vacations, we went on boat rides and rode jet skis. You had overnight kids' parties with new friends. You got to see lightning bugs and tour places we never would have gone to see otherwise, because they weren't exactly vacation destinations. When you were young you also traveled without your dad and me. You traveled with your grandma Joanie (Dad's mom) to see your cousins once a year. I'm so thankful for how you bonded with your relatives on those trips.

There's one trip I remember especially clearly. You were ten years old and the family of one of your best friends had been planning a trip to Disneyland for quite a while. They asked you to go with them. You were all set. The trip was to take place in October 2001. You were super excited and ready to have fun in sunny Southern California. Then the twin towers were bombed—9/11. We knew that teaching you fear was *not* an option. So, we let you go. Until you left and while you were gone I really needed to trust and have faith that your journey would be safe and full of fun.

I also knew that preparing you for the world and fostering your independence required a series of small steps on all our parts, and that with each step you took, you'd gain a few more tools to take with you on your next journey. When you broke your wrist on the playground and later broke the other one, you cried less the second time because you'd already been through the experience and knew that the pain would eventually go away.

Adding to your toolbox was kind of like that, only you might not gain your tools through such a painful experience. Your dad and I felt that the trip to Disneyland was an important step. You'd be traveling with another family, without your dad, me, or your grandma. I remember a friend of ours being astonished that we'd let you go on an airplane trip without us right after 9/11. Believe me, it wasn't easy. Of course, we wouldn't have let you go if we believed you would be in danger. Still, I used every ounce of courage I had, locking up my fear and placing it on the tippy-top shelf of the closet while you were gone.

Boy, I'm glad we taught you to recognize people who might have ill intentions, to be cautious, and listen to your gut about situations and people that could be threatening. I'm glad we taught you to trust and believe in good and not live in fear, because this internal faith has made your life so much richer. Facing and overcoming fear is one of our challenges as human beings. As Eleanor Roosevelt said, "Do one thing every day that scares you." We wanted to make sure you knew how to make good choices, take on life-altering experiences, and live a fearless life. This did not mean that we taught you to do things that were reckless.

Carly, you'll find out only when and if you become a parent how hard it is to put fear away. There are times when it's taken an iron will on my part to put worry out of my mind and replace it with trust and faith. But I did so, because I believe that when you let fear direct your life, you're no longer in charge, and you run the risk of letting outside influences govern your life. So, make sure that you're extremely mindful about recognizing when fear is a warning to be listened to, and when it's an anxiety about a new situation. If it's anxiety, I urge you to overcome that fear and go for it!

There's a quotation by Marianne Williamson that I love: "Love is what we are born with. Fear is what we learn. The spiritual journey is the unlearning of fear and prejudice and the acceptance of love back into our hearts." I recall one of our recent conversations when you told me that, when I was worried about somewhere you were traveling, my worry wouldn't stop you from exploring the world and it would not keep you safe. Great point, my dear. Just a hard one to be mindful of sometimes.

I'm glad that we taught you this very point, and that you took it in. I'm also really grateful you reminded me. When writing this book, you and I had several conversations about your childhood. I wanted to understand some of your perceptions so that I could fill in any blanks. Just in case you've forgotten our recent exchange, here are some questions along with your answers (pretty interesting stuff from you at twenty-two):

When you were growing up did I make you think you had to be perfect?

> No, I knew that nobody was perfect. That is the beautiful diversity of humanity.

Did we allow you to struggle?

> Yes, you did allow me to struggle while conversing about the struggle and potential ways to deal with it.

Did you feel worthy of love and belonging?

> Yes, I always felt worthy. I also knew that everyone around me was worthy of love and belonging.

Did you feel accountable for the effect that you had on others?

> Yes, I knew that my actions influenced the external environment and that its INFLUENCE WAS IN PART MY RESPONSIBILITY.

Did you feel like you belonged?

> Yes, I felt I was an integral and vital part of my family and of the larger human community.

Do you feel like you are enough?

> Yes, I am consistently involving myself in the everyday to the best of my abilities and that is enough.

Your answers really impressed me, and I'd like to think that your sense of self was in part fueled by your travels and experiences. Many of the world's people are not as blessed with food, shelter, and clothing as we are.

I recall one of the people who had a profound impact on your life—Dickey, the six year old orphan girl you met when you spent three weeks volunteering at an orphanage in Tibet. You were part of a group of girls led by your soccer coach, his daughter, and a few other parents. I know seeing Dickey's situation took your understanding of the difference between "need" and "want" to a new level. Your life was filled with such abundance that you had all that you needed, even if there were things you wanted or desired. Then you saw this little girl who didn't even have what she needed, let alone what she might want. And her idea of what she might want could be quite different from the privileged, first-world, Western ideal you'd been surrounded by while growing up.

I've often heard you speak about the over-consumption that we practice in America, and I think your eyes began to open on that trip. As you've grown up, I love that you've become clearer every day about your consumption, about what you need and what you buy. I love that you look at labels, because you won't buy things manufactured in sweatshops. I love that you don't buy on the spur of the moment, that you decide in advance about whether you really need that new/used item. And, I love that you spend the majority of your income on supporting socially responsible businesses.

When you returned from your three weeks in Tibet, we were happy that you'd come home safe and sound, and we were equally happy about the changes in you, how much you'd grown as a human being. You learned profound lessons on that journey without us, lessons that I believe will stick with you for your entire life. Just so you know, I would've loved to have gone with you on that adventure, but I knew it was time for you to test your wings, to begin your own journey.

While exploring the world, you've learned that many people have much different perspectives from those we have in our country. They have some awesome ways of living and some not so awesome. When traveling, you prepared well, adjusted your expectations, used your street smarts, and kept in mind that hate and fear are too heavy a load to carry, so you didn't pack them in your suitcase. I trust you will continue to traverse the earth and you'll take your child/children along with you. I have every confidence that your wide array of adventures will continue.

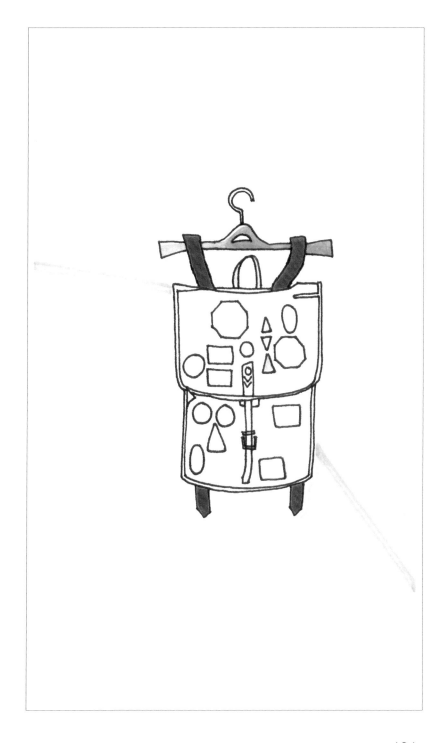

Something else to remember, it's super important to give your kids the tools they'll need to succeed before you send them out exploring. You want to make sure that you don't set them up for failure. If you give them tools that are age-appropriate along the way, then each new step can become their success.

Birth through age two

When you were first born, Dad and I thought that our ideal nanny would have been raised in a foreign country and speak English as a second language. Lucky for us, a friend had the perfect connection to Maffe, who spoke Spanish to you all day long. She also read to you from Spanish children's books, an experience you both enjoyed.

Throughout your childhood, we focused on guiding you toward independence. We intuitively knew that if you understood how to explore safely, you'd have an easier time reaching that goal. So when you were small, we helped you explore the world through the influence of family, friends, babysitters, and nanny sharing. The neighborhood families helped you learn how to explore with children your own age as did co-op preschool. You were always so curious, and we encouraged your curiosity.

There were so many loved ones surrounding

us that it was easy for you to explore in different ways. Grandma Carol and Grandpa Lin liked to show you how to explore your world through books, Grandpa Marlin and Grandma Anita (Dad's father and his stepmom) had you explore with tents, forts, and the world of make believe. Daddy liked to help you explore the world by "flying" you through the air, seeing all that you could while whooshing at "high" speeds. You two would go whizzing through the house and yard with him holding you up in the air with his arms raised holding you tightly.

In my office, I have a photo of you when you were about eighteen months old. You have a wide grin on your face and you're pointing to a little bug. You learned a lot about insects and their world from watching bugs. Our cats and dogs also helped you learn about their world.

Studying the different worlds of our neighbors, family, school, insects, and animals, not to mention seeing it from the air, broadened your horizons, and helped you to understand different outlooks and ways of doing things. We tried to help you understand different points of view and what we knew about different cultures. (And, you know me, I tried to help others understand as well.) We were always excited to learn something new, and we were clear about wanting to expose you to as many experiences as we could so that you would learn acceptance and not fear.

Ages three through five

I was talking about this book with a customer the other day and he started singing his mother's praises. She was a teacher and (in his words) an amazing, natural, and adept mother. He said that when he was a child, she let him explore the world while she monitored his safety from "afar."

Here's how it went. They had a really long driveway that he was allowed to play on, but he had to stay in an area that was determined by the sideline of the driveway. His mother would hide around the corner so he couldn't see her. Whenever he strayed outside the boundary, she'd appear. She would remind him of the rule about staying on the driveway and make sure he understood.

After a few times of her reminding him, he got it. What a great way to prepare your kids for success. To me, it's brilliant when parents combine borders with exploration. Another reason her method worked was that she was consistent, which helped him learn rules and borders. Her method was a lot of work, it's true. Enforcing rules and teaching independence can be super hard and wear a person down, so take care to have all of the extra energy you'll need to be a parent. (See the chapter about nurturing your body and soul ☺.)

Your dad and I like to be active and we generally like to make the most of our time, so when you were small and could walk, you were about eleven months old, we would explore here, there, and everywhere. About this time, we were gifted a tandem bike with a Burley trailer behind it and we set off to explore. We learned a lot on that bike. Dad had to learn to ride a bike that was way longer than he was used to. We learned to communicate, so that we could have fun instead of frustrating ourselves because we were so busy figuring out how to navigate that we couldn't hold a conversation. Once we established a way of signaling where we wanted to go and how to work together to propel the bike forward, we had a great time. We loved exploring new places by bicycle and trailer.

Here's another wonderful scene I remember as though it were yesterday. We went to a wild game park over in Sequim. Huge buffalo, who were somewhat tame and safe, roamed the park. Visitors drove through the park in their cars, observing the animals from their vehicles. Your dad drove for a bit, and then we parked our van to watch. You were standing in the front seat between your dad and me. Dad had his car window open and a buffalo came up and stuck his head in the window. That buffalo had the worst breath ever! Boy howdy did you fly into the back, where you knew you'd be safe. For us, exploring meant safe, interesting experiences.

As I've said a number of times so far, safety was a big issue for us. We wanted you to explore safely, and take risks while exercising caution. While encouraging you to explore and take risks, we taught you to speak up if someone or something was troubling you. If you were out exploring with someone and we weren't with you, we needed to know that you'd speak up if there was a problem.

When you were about four, this understanding of safety and speaking out was tested. I can't go into details about the incident here for many reasons, but you learned that if you needed to tell someone that you didn't like what they were doing or you didn't feel safe, speaking up loud and clear was a great tool. In that instance, Daddy and I needed to intervene, but we talked at fairly great length about how you could protect yourself when you were in the presence of those who tested your boundaries. You learned that we would listen and that we trusted you to tell us when you felt unsafe. And, you saw that you could trust us to protect you.

On to the more fun adventures. By sharing a nanny, we increased our number of family passes to most Seattle kid-friendly places, so you kids all explored the zoo (which I know you're no longer a fan of—taking animals from their natural habitat and caging them or raising their offspring in captivity), the aquarium, the Pacific Science Center, and your personal favorite, the Seattle Children's Museum. All of you *loved* the land of make believe. And Shelli, your nanny, was great about encouraging your imagination and your world of make believe.

She also helped you kids set up your lemonade stands for early lessons in business. I loved the stands you kids created. Each one was really pretty with a bright tablecloth and colorful signs. Not only were you great designers but you were pretty savvy about business. When it came to determining what to charge, you all found out that writing "Pay whatever you like," on the sign earned you way more money. A stroke of brilliance. I have no idea how you, Rory (one of the kids with whom you shared a nanny), and Shelli arrived at this pricing strategy, but it sure generated a lot more money than if you'd charged a set price.

I want to reiterate how important it is to find the right care person or care center. Maybe it's a co-op. Just so your kids can be with other kids, explore, and be creative. Be kids. By nanny sharing, we were able to afford to have Shelli watch you kids. You all went here, there, and everywhere for fun adventures throughout the day. From my perspective, she helped to give you a blessed, magical childhood.

Ages six through ten

When you started elementary school, you were gifted with many ways to explore. You learned a bit about other cultures and languages. Because the population was so diverse, you learned how to approach familiar tasks in new ways, and you were in a safe environment. At around this age, you began to start exploring sports and teamwork.

By spending the night at your friends' homes, you learned about new family dynamics and traditions. Among other things, these overnights helped you learn to prepare for trips. We taught you how to pack a bag. You learned to make a list and you learned the natural consequence of forgetting something that you meant to bring along. You knew when you forgot something, you usually had to deal with it on your own. We rarely rescued you by bringing the forgotten item to you.

You also went places that we felt would be safe places for you to start exploring alone. Each year, the parameters grew. When there were problems or misunderstandings, you would come home and we'd talk about how you might have solved the problem. Or, if it were still unresolved, we discussed what you could do about it. We talked over what might happen if you ran into a similar situation in the future. Either way, we discussed whether you could handle the issues alone or if we needed to help. We always had your back and were open to conversation. Much of the time, you handled the issue and grew from the interaction. As parents, we thought we should encourage your independence and ability to grow through the bumpy roads.

I remember a time when you and your best friend from the neighborhood were at our house and got into a fight. This time I was around, so it wasn't a situation we were going to discuss later. Your friend was ready to storm out, and you were all too happy to see her go. I asked you girls to resolve the disagreement before she went home. I don't think either of you liked this solution, but I know you both grew from this experience. You learned that walking out on a problem isn't going to solve it. You also learned more about reconciling differences.

It was during these years that your dad started taking you to work with him on some Saturdays. Another way to explore life. You learned more about doing a job well and the benefits of hard work. Dad had you sanding cars. You also worked on other projects that he was working on at his auto-body shop. I think it helped you figure out what tasks you liked and which ones you didn't.

The adventures that you went on with your dad at his work also helped you to develop a great work ethic. The practice continued at home. You sanded our doors before we painted them. Speaking of which, I believe kids can develop a good work ethic by learning manual labor while when they're young. Whether you build a birdhouse, weed a bed of flowers, or sand a door, it's extremely satisfying to see the fruits of your labor become something concrete.

During these years, you were also learning how to communicate quite well without us. It was really cool to watch you connecting with your peers, teachers, and mentors. When we made the decision for you to try private school, you went to a neighbor and several teachers to get letters of recommendation. You gained the experience of asking for help from a community who loved you. There are so many ways to explore the world and you jumped in with both feet most of the time.

Ages eleven through thirteen

Until you were twelve years old, we hired babysitters to watch you when your dad and I went out on date night. (We loved date night! And you loved your babysitters. Wow. Now that you've left the nest, I think we need to reestablish those date nights. What a great reminder!)

You had many fabulous babysitters as a child. Amy and Dana were great at babysitting and teaching you how to become a fun, confident babysitter. Babysitting is a great way to explore and build confidence, and your babysitters provided a great model for when you were ready to babysit other kids.

You prepared yourself to babysit by attending a babysitting class to learn how to do your best. I think you learned the basics of first aid, what to do in emergency situations, and what things you should know before the parents headed out the door. You learned the lessons well and had a long list of clients to prove it.

You also learned how to make new friends and new mentors as you went to two new schools during this time, a skill that's served you well as you've traversed the world with your studies. As your mom, I was very determined to find you great schools with engaging teachers who were excited about teaching.

Here's what I learned. Your teachers were a mixed bag. While inspiring, fun teachers were the ideal, you had some who were dull and boring, and that was okay. There is no perfect school, but changing schools was not the BIG deal that I worried it would be. Sometimes I think parents need to get out of our adult perspective and follow the lead of watching how our kids react to new settings. You did great at both schools. I know that both schools were sorry to see you move on.

At this age, as you'll remember, I left my great paying job to follow a dream and give back to our community. Not my best financial decision, but when something speaks to your heart, it will speak much louder than money, and when you hear that call, follow it. When I opened the non-profit for foster parents and foster kids, we had no idea of the impact this decision would have on our family. You and your father gave a TON of volunteer hours. My hat's off to you both. I know that our family gained more than we gave during this huge volunteer effort.

While volunteering, you met a variety of folks who helped to shape the way you looked at the world. I think giving of your time helped you to understand the importance of the community of family, and to understand the many ways there are to define family.

When you were twelve, we were able to take a trip to Europe and to show you more of the world on a Mediterranean cruise. In hindsight, it might have been a good idea if your dad and I had taken this trip earlier, maybe on our honeymoon, but we were restricted by finances. Had we taken the trip earlier, I think your dad would have had a better understanding about the opinions I expressed during discussions about U.S. politics.

Until that trip, when we talked about ways to improve the U.S., your dad (and others) thought I was unpatriotic. After the trip, he understood where I was coming from, because he was able to see how others solved issues plaguing the U.S., and he then understood my thoughts about potential improvements we could make in our country. I know that I learned these lessons when I was young while living in Europe. It would have been nice to have us on this same page earlier in our marriage.

Your viewpoint expanded along with his on our trip. You explored more foods and different ways of dining. You saw new rhythms of life, perspectives, and traditions. It was also interesting to watch how each member of our family experienced new opportunities so differently.

Remember how our cruise boat stopped in Tunisia and how much daddy didn't like the carpet market and how comfortable you and I were there? I think your dad felt he needed to keep both of us safe, while you and I saw a chance to explore. Good that dad kept a watchful eye, and great that we got to explore.

This trip was a game changer for our family on so many levels. Travel is such a gift, as you know. I'm sure that your love of travel and exploration fueled your decision to work on your master's degree in South Africa.

Ages fourteen through eighteen

When I think of your high school years, I remember how you traveled and experienced different ways of living by taking five big trips, mostly without us. Tibet was the first trip when you were fourteen years old. Tibet changed your life. It changed how you perceived our country, how you thought about one country overpowering another, and what a REALLY huge foreign city could look like.

Beijing was a real eye opener for you; I remember you talked about the taxi driver who was trying to cheat you and your friend by taking a convoluted route to rack up the miles. You yelled at him, telling him you knew he was swindling you and you weren't going to pay the extra fare. You were definitely growing up and speaking your truth. Though I have to admit, when you called and told me the story, it scared the hell out of me.

While writing this book, I asked you to comment about how you felt each of these trips impacted you. You said, "Tibet is where I fell in love with exploration, beyond the bugs in our gardens and local beaches. It was a heartwarming and heartbreaking journey. Because I knew very little Tibetan, I learned quickly that humans can connect in ways that language does not allow. As I sat in a psychiatric ward with Dickey, my orphaned friend, she dug her nails into the palms of my hands and her tears fell onto her crisscrossed legs. Her innocence had been stripped away from her through a childhood of abuse. She was just a little girl, and I was fourteen, but she taught me more than I could ever imagine."

The second big trip you took was for a summer semester at The Fashion Institute of Technology in Manhattan when you were fifteen years old. At that time, you were considering a career in fashion design and wanted to explore the idea. When we enrolled you in the course, we were told that you weren't old enough to stay in the dorms, so we devised an alternative plan.

I flew to New York with you, took you to the school, and stayed with you for a few days until you got the hang of traveling back and forth by bus and train from your Aunt Wendy and Uncle Angel's home in New Jersey to the FIT campus in Manhattan. You love your aunt and uncle, so being able to spend time with them was perfect.

Then I headed back to Seattle. During that time, if you needed anything, you turned to your aunt and uncle, but for the most part, you were self-sufficient. A couple weeks later, your dad and I flew to the East Coast to view your art show and fly home with you. During the time I spent at the school, I saw so many helicopter moms. You know the ones. They never give their kids a second to breathe on their own or to learn how to fail or to succeed on their own. To find a balance in parenting, to steer clear of extremes—what a great thing for parents to model for their kids.

Recently, I asked you how you felt about that trip. You wrote, "New York was overwhelming. FIT felt cold and institutional and the mechanization of life extended beyond its campus. Navigating my way through the trains and buses that took me to and from New Jersey to the City daily was a vast methodical maze—almost mind numbing. Regardless, through my newly acquired independence, without Seattle friends and family, I left New York feeling accomplished, grown, and capable."

When you wanted to go into fashion design and headed off to FIT, I did my best to keep my mouth shut. As you know fashion and all of its trappings are not my thing. Still, your dad and I did our best to support you while you explored this possibility.

When you were seventeen and decided to explore fashion further by going to Providence, Rhode Island for a six-week, pre-college course at the Rhode Island School of Design (RISD), I wasn't thrilled. But I realized I'd done a decent job of supporting you despite my views. I think I may have been mindful in this area because of the lack of support that your grandma Carol got from her parents when she wanted to be a makeup artist. I still hear the disappointment and regret in her voice when she speaks of it. Who knows what her life may have looked like if she'd followed her dreams?

So, off you went on your third big trip. I took you there, went back home, and then flew out to fly home with you. Boy was that a big adventure. During that trip, you stayed in the dorms. You learned how to deal with an unfortunate roommate. You saw what hard-work and self-motivation entailed, and what it looked like for those who really, really wanted to become fashion designers. It was an incredible experience for you.

Here's what you had to say: "Providence was my playground for the summer of 2008. Confident in my knowledge about apparel, I approached these incredible six weeks with enthusiasm and drive. I went in wanting my own fashion label more than anything. When I left, I wanted anything but that. I worked harder in those six weeks than I ever have since. All the hard work left me questioning the social importance of clothes. I trusted in my creativity but not in the satisfaction of twenty-four hour days dedicated to the design, production, and manufacturing of stuff."

The other two trips were with your Spanish

class. Both times you went to Central America. You said, "Costa Rica, in both my sophomore and senior year of high school, exemplified the fun in travel— the lighthearted reality that the world can only be as serious as we make it. I was with my best friends in a warm, sunny, and festive tourist environment. I ate sugar cane, planted trees, and mostly laughed my way through Central America. I was traveling, but I didn't feel far from home. Home was then, and is now, the people that surround me."

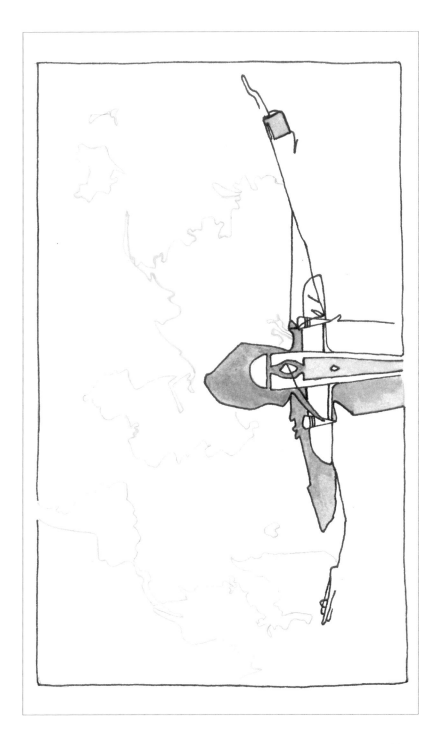

You had become a world traveler. It was just what you needed. You certainly got the hang of packing. You learned how to speak up, immerse yourself in different cultures, be of help to others when you traveled, and to leave someplace better then you found it. I'm sure that if you sat down to write a list of what you learned during these years you might surprise yourself.

I could go on and on about how you explored the world during high school, but I think it might be more interesting for you to rehash these lessons. What I know to be true is that we did our best to provide opportunities for you to succeed and fail. When you wanted to travel, we always made sure you had skin in the game by working to help fund these trips. We had lively conversations about anything and everything, so that you could make sound decisions. We taught you to trust others as well as yourself, and we gave you freedom as you earned it. You were very trustworthy and earned every bit of our faith in you.

Carly's Soul Searching

Carly, when you read an early draft of this book, you were shocked that I'd left out this story, which was a pivotal point in your life, one I'd forgotten completely, and one I'm still fuzzy about. I'm including it here, because it's important.

You were in middle school. One morning, when I was in the shower, you knocked at the door and then burst into the bathroom, sobbing. We needed to talk, you said. I asked if we could talk later (maybe when I could actually hear you and pay attention?). You said, "No."

Worried, I asked if you needed me to get out of the shower right then and finish bathing later. Again you said, "No." I think you chose that moment —when we were separated by a curtain, and the shower muffled your words—because you felt safe telling me something that you knew you'd done wrong. "What's going on?" I asked you. Crying even harder, you told me you'd done some really BAD things . . . more than once. You'd faked being sick, you'd ditched class, and you'd cheated at math.

As you continued to sob, I reminded you what I thought of lying and moving your ethical markers. I asked you how you'd felt when you'd done those things. You'd felt bad, you said. But at that moment, you felt far worse. I don't know why it all hit you so hard that morning. I'm not sure you do either.

When you reminded me of this story, you were extremely frustrated with me and couldn't understand how I could forget such a pivotal moment in your life. I think that this moment loomed so large in your memory, because for the first time, on your own, you'd taken a hard look at yourself and you didn't like what you saw. But I saw that you felt true remorse. You'd done some things that were very wrong, had hidden the wrong-doing, and released all the pent up energy by telling the truth to make sure you wouldn't continue the behavior.

Your actions were wrong, but by coming to me with the truth, you showed sorrow about letting yourself down. I saw you had learned the lessons for lying and cheating and were punishing yourself enough for both of us so I moved on.

Recently, you also told me you'd cheated again at math during the first two years of high school, so you know that we don't always learn our lessons the first time. Or the second, or...

And, when you've learned the lesson, you'll find new ones (I'm sure you've learned plenty that you haven't told me about). We're humans. We make mistakes. It's what we do. I know you've drawn on that moment in the bathroom to help you get through other lessons you've learned, and I know you'll draw on that moment to get through those coming challenges.

And now, because I've written it down, I, too, will always remember this moment when you learned to search your heart. It takes a lot of courage to look at ourselves so deeply, and to change. You did it, and you continue to do it. I so respect that about you.

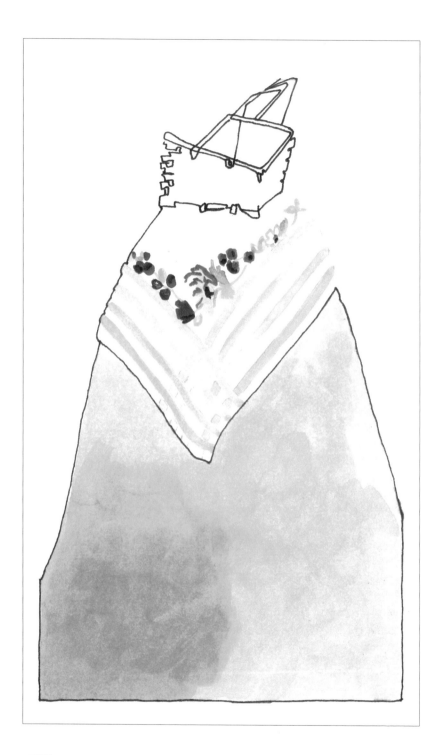

A Few Last Thoughts, Kiddo

We taught you that each person on this planet is special. They have a place at the table and something to share. We also taught you to be cautious of those who are harmful and bury their light so deep that *they* can't even find it. Know that not everyone will want a place at your table, no matter how beautifully it's set, even with all the yummy food you'll provide. Keep looking for the gifts in other people, and stay open to all they have to teach you.

As you grow older, you'll realize that you have more questions than answers. I'm very clear that we didn't do everything right or perfect and there are many other ways to parent than the ways we chose. There's no need for you to be right or perfect all the time. But I do trust you'll be open to finding your parenting path (once again, should you choose this road) by listening to the wisdom of others, trusting your heart, and cherishing your child for who he or she is. I also know you'll be an absolutely open, conscious, and consistent parent. Above all else, I hope you've enjoyed receiving *The Invisible Parenting Handbook* and reminiscing about your childhood.

It's been our pleasure and honor to be your parents, Carly. There's no greater joy for us than to see what an amazing human being you've become.

I look forward to watching all the ways you'll touch others in this world, and I imagine I'll get to continue to watch you volunteering for causes you're passionate about and initiating positive changes the world so desperately needs.

I have hope that your generation will more than make up for the failings of past generations, most recently, of course, mine. I've been inspired watching you and your friends "Make Great Choices." I trust that your generation will find that greed, power, and unethical behavior can only make everyone's lives meaningless. And I trust you'll explore your options, search for the truth, and love and cherish this planet we're so lucky to live on. Thanks to you and your friends for living such authentic lives. And thank you, Carly, for teaching us as much as I believe we've taught you.

Love,

Mom and Dad

About Mama — A Daughter's Perspective

Sometimes my mom flies through this world like a gale-force wind. One evening, when I was fourteen, she practically leapt into my bedroom. She did this a lot—leaping through my door, embracing life with a sort of wild, childlike abandon. "You get to go to Tibet!" she exclaimed. So in the summer of 2006, still fourteen, I waved goodbye to my parents at the SeaTac airport, and boarded a plane to Beijing en route to Lhasa.

A year later, I was on a plane again, on my way to a summer program at the Fashion Institute of Technology in New York City. Mom flew out with me, helped me get the lay of the Island, and then flew back home. I was left to my own devices in one of the world's largest cities. For two weeks I travelled back and forth by bus and train from my aunt and uncle's home in New Jersey to the FIT campus in Manhattan.

I could go on, but what I'm ultimately trying to get across is that my mom shows her love through selfless encouragement. Both my parents sent me to Lhasa and New York understanding the educational role experience plays, and, most important, trusting me. I know my Mom is my biggest supporter. Bypassing compliments such as "You're smart" or "You're beautiful," my mother shows her love by facilitating my growth. She loves in a way that surpasses physical proximity.

Sometimes when I think about my mother, I imagine her carrying these big baskets full of people, me included. Not because we need her to hold us up, but because she chooses to take us under her wings regardless. Sitting in my Grahamstown, South Africa bedroom, I can still feel her wings stretching from Seattle to nurture and encourage me. To call her a people person would be an unfortunate understatement. In fact, I've never met a person who is more unassuming, outspoken, genuine, supportive and welcoming in my life.

Carly

Dear Readers,

I've included the revised version of our Carly List on the next two pages. The qualities we hoped she'd embrace for her trip through life follow that. Feel free to copy these to post on your own fridge. Or, better yet, create some of your own. Your goals and aspirations may greatly differ from Mark's and mine.

I hope you have come away with plenty of ideas and interesting things to consider as you venture forth along this bouncy, bumpy road called parenthood!

Our (Revised) Carly List

- Maintain connections with the important people in Carly's life for continuity and to build a solid foundation of community
- Assign chores for responsibility
- Make sure she savors childhood, so she doesn't grow up too fast
- Have her work part-time jobs for clothes, college savings, and fun
- Avoid spoiling Carly with big-ticket items such as cars, to teach her the value of honest work and a dollar
- Steer clear of junk TV and junk food
- Promote reading—very important
- Allow no video games
- Take vacations together
- Make sure there are plenty of positive influences in Carly's life

- Teach her to have fun and be responsible about safety, without becoming frightened of risks
- Instill manners so that she can travel in any circle comfortably
- Encourage participation in sports, if she's interested
- Limit the use of cosmetics
- Veto unreasonable clothing or jewelry
- Instill spiritual values (not religious)
- Follow through on thank you notes
- Talk with each other. Hold meaningful conversations.
- Develop moral values and social awareness.
- Foster a sense of gratitude for what you have rather than entitlement to what you don't have.

HONESTY INTEGRITY COMPASSION
RESPECT FOR YOURSELF & OTHERS
RESPONSIBILITY CONFIDENCE
SELF-SUFFICIENCY AUTHENTICITY
OF SERVICE TO YOUR COMMUNITY
PASSION CURIOSITY
COURAGE
MANNERS g WORLD STEWARDSHIP
FAITH ABILITY TO DIG
CAPACITY FOR CONVERSATION D
& ability TO LISTEN E
APTITUDE TO FIND OR IN A STORM E
HEEDING THE OF OTHERS P
WISDOM
OPENNESS SATISFACTION
GRATITUDE